TALES
FROM
GREAT
PASSENGER
SHIPS

TALES
FROM
GREAT
PASSENGER
SHIPS

A JAUNT THROUGH TIME

PAUL CURTIS

The
History
Press

'Fair Winds and Following Seas ...'
(Anon)

The sailors' traditional wish for good luck
for your ongoing voyage through life.

Front cover image: Cunard's RMS *Queen Mary* and RMS *Queen Elizabeth* ocean
liners. (WorldPhotos/Alamy Stock Photo)

First published 2023

The History Press
97 St George's Place, Cheltenham,
Gloucestershire, GL50 3QB
www.thehistorypress.co.uk

British Library Cataloguing in Publication Data.
A catalogue record for this book is available from the British Library.

ISBN 978 1 80399 211 2

Typesetting and origination by The History Press
Printed and bound in Great Britain by TJ Books Limited, Padstow, Cornwall.

Trees for LYfe

Contents

(Ships Listed in Order of End of Life)

Author's Note

'Now hear this ...'

I borrow this nautical phrase, commonly used by the US Navy to call sailors to 'listen up', to explain why, in this often-personal account of the life of a ship, I have used the somewhat whimsical terms 'born' and 'died' rather than the more mundane and commonly used 'launched' and 'scrapped'.

Why? Well, I love ships. They may well be tons of metals heaped and welded together in a maze of stacked steel plates, but to me they are living, breathing beings. Life is poured into them by the hearts and sweat of everyone from welders, carpenters, electricians, engineers and designers to the crew and passengers who, in all weathers, journey on them for work or play. They are, in fact, floating homes.

So many of us have walked into a house and sensed this is a happy place: that this home has a presence, and this home has character.

You can get this strange sensation of another dimension when you walk into some small church in a devout community. Even cathedrals can give off a similar vibe, if they are not plagued with thousands of snapping and flashing cameras and the walls not cluttered with endless vanity oil portraits glorifying past priests.

I am not the only person given to the personification of loved items. I have a friend who has lived in several countries but always takes with him an antique Queen Anne dining table – not the easiest thing to keep lugging around the world. Over many decades he has taken it wherever he is sent.

To him, his table is alive with recollections of great dinners and conversations and he calls his table 'she'.

And so, we refer to boats and ships as 'she'. And if 'she' is to have a life on this planet, she must be born. To my mind, her true birthday is the day she bursts from the womb with all fingers and toes accounted for and sets off on her maiden voyage.

And when she dies, as she surely must, like all of us, we do not say we are sending her to the undertakers to be scrapped. In line with afterlife theories, she is recycled and bits of her become something else. Maybe the car you are driving contains steel from one of the great ocean liners.

I can be called out as drawing a long bow. But you either sense these things or you do not. What further justification can I offer?

Also, an eagle-eyed reader with the memory of an elephant may recognise three of my stories on the Cunard Queens include some small anecdotal extracts from my book *High Tea on the Cunard Queens*. *Mea culpa*. But I definitely think they are worth retelling. So there!

Common Nautical Terms Explained

Aft	Towards the stern of a ship.
Air Height	Measured from the waterline to the topmost point of the ship.
Amidships	Midpoint of the distance between bow and stern.
Beam	The width of the ship from side to side at its widest point.
Companionway	On a ship this refers to the stairway from one deck to another.
Cruise Ship vs Liner	A liner is a ship that maintains a regular schedule on a route to a distant port. They are built with reinforced and finer bows to cope with severe weather conditions experienced in all seasons. A cruise ship makes voyages for pleasure with a variable route and is designed for excellent accommodation and the ability to change routes to avoid severe weather. The only proper liner left is the *Queen Mary 2*. The only other passenger ships running a regular schedule are more likely to be on short runs and called ferries.
Draft	The depth below the waterline to the bottom of the keel.

Fathoms	The depth of the water is measured in fathoms. It is an old English way of measuring and refers to the distance of a man with arms outstretched between fingertips to fingertips. In other words (approximately) 6ft.
Forward	Any point on the ship that is towards the bow when facing the front of the ship.
GRT	Gross Registered Tonnage. This has nothing to do with the actual weight, it is a measurement of the amount of available space for passengers and does not include crew quarters and engine rooms.
Hull	The watertight body of a ship.
Knots (kt)	A unit of speed to cover one nautical mile in one hour. A nautical mile is 6,080.3ft. Why such an odd measure? Well, that distance is one minute of arc on a circle of the earth. So it all makes sense from a navigational point of view.
Length	The distance between the most forward part of the ship and the very end, known as the stern. It is the length overall. Sometimes referred to as LOA.
Port	Left side of the ship when facing forward.
Screw	A ship's propeller.
Ship Prefixes	Commonly used are terms such as MS (Motor Ship); MV (Motor Vessel); RMS (Royal Mail Ship); SS (single-screw ship); TSS (twin-screw ship); TSMS (twin-screw motor ship); TEL (Turbo Electric Drive); RN (Royal Navy) and USS (United States Ship). Finally, just in case, know the prefix LB means it's the ship's lifeboat.
Sister Ships	Sometimes used to refer to vessels in the same line, it is used in this book to refer to near identical ships from the same line.
Starboard	Right-hand side of the ship when facing forward.

Stern	The very back of the ship.
Waterline	The floating line where the hull meets the water. The different salinity of the various seas can affect the buoyancy of a ship, so there can be several lines on the bow of a ship to mark the limits of loading for the various seas. These are known as Plimsoll Lines.

How Safe is Cruising?

Included in this book are a few ships that met unfortunate ends. This is partly because I have selected ships with a history: not many biographies are written on the lives of 3-year-olds. So, while some of the selected ships met calamity, they are not included just to entertain and titillate. They are here because they earned their place in history and most definitely should not give a false impression of the true safety of cruising. The fact is that even with the hundreds of ships now cruising the world, it is the safest form of holiday travel.

Media tales of the sea include horror stories of people contracting Covid-19, being hit by horrendous storms, ships sinking, pirate attacks, terrorists, murders and waves of norovirus-sick passengers. The truth is these circumstances are so unusual they ensure intensive and disproportionate media coverage. If it happens, it's going to be big news. Indeed, the sinking of *Titanic* is still making news and it happened far more than a century ago.

Compared to flying, on a ship, if you are ever involved in some sort of crash, you still have a good chance of survival. Whereas when an aircraft hits the deck, it's mostly a case of candles in the wind.

Fear of pirates should not deter you. Although equipped with fast, small boats, a 2019 report said only 6 of the 230 recorded attacks by young men armed to the teeth with AK-47s were against cruise ships. None of these were successful. In more recent years, the number of attacks on shipping has diminished greatly due to an international navy presence in key areas such as the Gulf of Aden, Indonesia and parts of India in the Arabian Sea.

Today, all cruise ships are geared up to deal with any attempts by deploying everything from barbed wire, high-powered water hoses, ear-splitting sonic boom equipment and, when in high-risk areas, military-trained snipers. When a ship is passing through such places, passengers can be sent to special assembly areas where they are totally protected. Of those few passenger ships attacked, even the smallest, the under 100-ton *Seabourn Spirit*, in 2005 saw them off safely by firing a sonic boom gun.

The term piracy is generally used to refer to attacks on ships in international waters, and is defined as an assault with the purpose of making financial gain. Terrorism, on the other hand, is when the motivating factor is either religious or political.

However, terrorism has so far been less of a threat at sea than we experience in many of our cities on land. Due to the vastness of the oceans and weather conditions, even finding a particular ship can be difficult. During the Second World War, the combined might of the Nazi war machine could not manage to catch either RMS *Queen Mary* or RMS *Queen Elizabeth*. This was despite a huge bounty offered on both their heads.

In 1973, when *Queen Elizabeth 2* (*QE2*) was on a Mediterranean cruise to Israel to mark its twenty-fifth anniversary of foundation, Muammar Gaddafi let it be known he planned to sink the famous ship with a submarine as revenge for the downing of Libyan Arab Airlines Flight 114. He was planning to borrow the submarine from Egypt, but the Egyptian president, Anwar Sadat, fearful of repercussions, countermanded the requisition.

Al-Qaeda also made threats to the maiden voyage of *Queen Mary 2* (*QM2*), but the ship's progress was protectively monitored and in ports patrol craft stood by. In Fort Lauderdale protective boom nets were deployed, preventing any possible close approaches by submerged craft or frogmen.

There has only been one hijacking of a passenger ship in recent times and that was of the Italian ship *Achille Lauro* in 1985 (see Chapter 21), but this really was a rare event.

The murder rate on cruise ships is also very low, especially when you consider the number of people in a confined area. Those on board are likely to be relaxed and having a good time, plus security is very tight and alcohol consumption is monitored closely. If a murder does happen, it makes very big media news indeed.

In instances of Covid-19 among those living in near proximity, there are millions more cases ashore than there have ever been at sea. Furthermore, because of the years of having to cope with the norovirus, ships are more experienced and better equipped to handle infectious disease outbreaks than many shore establishments. Blaring news headlines screamed about a gastro outbreak on board *Diamond Princess*, but the cold fact is it only affected 150 people out of the 4,000 on board. In the very early days of the discovery of Covid-19 on ships, *Ruby Princess* generated huge headlines for weeks when 133 people on board tested positive. But, while not wishing to be thought to be downplaying the matter, it is not so catastrophic when you consider there were again nearly 4,000 people on board. However, this combined with other ship outbreaks, was enough to put a brake on cruising for two years. There is a risk, but personally I don't think it is any worse than going to the theatre.

Storms, hurricanes, cyclones and freak waves are a more natural form of threat, but again, the ability of modern cruise ships to cope with such circumstances are a far different story from the harrowing tales of yester-year. For instance, the media leapt on a 2016 story of *Anthem of the Seas* encountering an extreme storm with terrible seas and 122mph winds off the notorious Cape Hatteras. The ship was on her return leg from the Bahamas to the New Jersey port of Bayonne. Watertight doors were closed and passengers were confined to their cabins as furniture was hurled around and water poured in through upper windows smashed by the waves. But of the 4,529 passengers on board only four were injured and none seriously.

The fact is that cruising is one of the safest holidays you can take. So, go cruise.

1

RMS *Britannia*

(Later SMS *Barbarossa*)

RMS *Britannia*.

Born	1840
Died	1880
GRT	1,154
Length	207ft
Beam	34ft
Speed	8.5 knots
Passengers	115
Crew	82
Line	Cunard Line
Sister ships	*Acadia*, *Caledonia* and *Columbia*

Pioneering Power on the Atlantic

The most famous and longest-established name in the shipping world could have been Kunder rather than Cunard. Probably just as well. Somehow Kunder doesn't have quit the same ring to it.

The Cunard family were Quakers, living in the English county of Worcestershire. In the seventeenth century, British authorities showed their disapproval of this religion by either jailing, evicting to penal colonies or confiscating their lands. I guess today you could call them extremists. But they were in charge. To escape this madness, the family took refuge in Germany, where they became known as the Kunders. Later, they moved on to Pennsylvania and reverted to the name of Cunard.

Despite this treatment in England, they remained loyal to the crown. Come the American Revolution, they transferred to Canada to continue living under the flag of the British Empire.

Samuel Cunard, born in 1787 and the founder of the shipping company, took a serious interest in the early use of steamships. He was an early adopter, ordering them for trading on his local Canadian waters.

Once firmly established in the shipping business, in 1837 he set off for England, seeking investors to form a company to bid for the rights to carry freight and the Royal Mail service between the United Kingdom and North America. He was successful and the North American Steam Packet Company was formed. This was mercifully shortened to Cunard Steamship Company. Nowadays, people just use 'Cunard'.

At the time, steam engines were not considered 100 per cent reliable, so many ships went for both sails and steam-driven power. Oddly enough, the idea of adding sails is slowly coming back into fashion for both passenger and cargo ships. With today's technology, adding some wind power is both economic and beneficial to the environment.

However, there was nothing environmental about coal-burning ships. Clouds of thick, black sooty smoke would spew from their funnels. Indeed, it is only recently that diesel-burning ships have stopped emitting dark clouds to trail in their wakes.

Britannia was the beginning of Cunard building its ships in Scotland, generally considered the home of engine-building prowess. When she was launched in 1840, she was a very large ship for her period. And to meet the rights to carry the Royal Mail she had to be of sufficient strength. *Britannia* also carried a proper armament of guns to protect both herself and British commerce on the seas. An example of 'Rule Britannia', and her determination to never, never, never be slaves.

Nowadays, Cunard has fun publishing her silhouette against that of their flagship *QM2* to show just how much their ships have grown. There is quite a difference between 149,000 and 1,154 tons. Yes, I know. It is 147,846. (I have a calculator.)

Britannia had a large wooden paddlewheel each side, driven by her steam engines, and three masts to support her sailing rig. Unlike sail-only ships, when the wind was light and in the right direction, she could power on and if the wind was strong enough, she could be propelled by wind power alone. In between times she could use both, but white sails were soon discoloured by the smoke from the funnels.

On her first run, she was carrying the prized Royal Mail, mixed cargo, 115 passengers, 82 crew and, to keep those paddle wheels turning, 600 tons of coal. The worst job on the ship was being a stoker. In fierce heat below they were constantly stoking coal into the fires to keep the boilers steaming.

There was a real fear of fire spreading and smoking was not allowed below decks, unless in the special smoking room. There was also a ladies-only saloon. This was to protect the ladies from both the smoke and unwanted advances.

First-class passengers were living in floating luxury. The fare of 35 guineas included unlimited wine and spirits. The restaurant took up most of the upper deck. Fresh eggs were provided by chickens housed in coops on the open deck. Between the two paddle wheels, a hut was home for the ship's cow. For the cow's protection against battering between the sides by the seas, the walls of the stable were thickly padded. Otherwise, the cow would be producing cottage cheese. The biggest fan of the cow's daily output was the ship's cat, earning its daily reward for the job of keeping rats at bay.

With the combination of steam and sail, on her maiden voyage *Britannia* made good time across the Atlantic, making it in just under twelve days and ten hours. On the return leg, with current and wind in her favour, she set a record, arriving in just under ten days at an average speed of 11 knots, or 12.6mph.

Seven years later, she was invited to take part in the first ocean race between British and American steamships. The American challenger was *Washington* – longer and with more power. They both left New York on the same day but *Britannia* reached England two days earlier.

Less impressed was Charles Dickens. Making an early crossing to the United States, he succumbed to a heavy bout of seasickness and exclaimed, 'This utterly impracticable, thoroughly hopeless, and profoundly preposterous box.'

He opted to return to Britain under sail.

Fellow writer Mark Twain took a more positive view of Cunard and wrote in his diary:

> The Cunard people would not take Noah himself until they have worked him through the lower grades and tried him for ten years. It takes them about ten years to manufacture a captain, but when they have him manu-factured to suit, at last they have full confidence in him.

Dickens had a change of heart when he later returned to Cunard for a voyage to the US on SS *Russia*. He wrote, 'The ship was fragrant with flowers and bubbles pervaded the nose.'

On one voyage, *Britannia* met a mishap in dense fog on the southern point of Newfoundland. A correspondent of the day wrote in the *New York Commercial Advertiser*:

> As you may imagine, it was a moment of deep solicitude. Many of us had been for some time watching for land, anxious to know our true situation, that we might escape all apprehension during the approaching night. My eye was at the moment fixed on Captain Harrison, our excel-lent commander, and I saw him turn quickly, and heard him exclaim, 'Starboard – stop her!' Before the echo could have died away the ship struck, and for the first time I saw the bleak and barren rocks.
>
> As soon as it was ascertained that the steamer was ashore, orders were given to clew up the sails, the guns were run aft, and the provisions and everything else that could be removed were shifted, the water in two of the boilers was let off, and the passengers all crowded to the stern; the engines were reversed, and two waves or rollers coming in, we were, under the gracious protection of an over-ruling Providence, once more afloat.
>
> The captain then summoned the chief engineer to ascertain whether the ship made water. The result was that she was making at the rate of about twelve inches per hour, but he was sure the two pumps usually in service would keep the water down. Under this impression the captain determined to proceed on his course.

The passengers, both ladies and gentlemen, behaved with great coolness during the exciting moment, and no one attempted to interfere with the commander in the course he pursued, nor did any one converse with him until we were again under way.

Soon after some half dozen gentlemen met the captain in his stateroom, and looked over his chart, and ascertained our position. St. John's was some fifty miles north of us, but as the fog still continued there was no probability of getting into that port, and having full confidence in Captain Harrison's statement, that the ordinary pumps would keep the ship free, Mr Winthrop made a report to the passengers which allayed their fears, and we arrived at Halifax on Friday morning, where a survey was held, and the report was made, in substance, that the steamer had been ashore at Newfoundland, that her forefoot had been knocked off, her keel injured, and that she made fourteen inches of water per hour; but that her two bilge pumps could throw out the water she made, and that she might proceed safely to Boston.

Now for the unusual part: sixty-five passengers got together on arrival in Boston and signed a statement attesting to the good judgement of the captain. That's something the captain of the *Costa Concordia* never managed after he hit the rocks. See the story in Chapter 29 of this book.

After making forty Atlantic crossings and holding the honour of being the first ship contracted to carry the Royal Mail, *Britannia*'s Cunard career ended in 1849. The company wanted to move on to newer ships and sold her to the German Confederation Navy, who named her SMS *Barbarossa*. They fitted her with nine guns, but these were never used against Britain. By 1880 she was so worn out she was used as a target ship for German gunners to practise their shooting.

The lamentable fact is this significant, pioneering ship of scheduled transatlantic crossings ended up blown to bits. A sad ending as *Britannia* had earned pride of place in any maritime museum.

2

RMS *Titanic*

RMS *Titanic*. (US National Archives/Heritage-Images/Imagestate)

Born	1912
Died	1912
GRT	46,328
Length	883ft
Beam	93ft
Passengers	2,435
Crew	892
Line	White Star Line
Sister ships	*Olympic, Britannic*

The Needless Tragedy

This should be a very short life story as *Titanic* died only five days out of the crib. However, the story of the 'unsinkable' *Titanic* is legendary. I hesitate to raise it again, so to speak, but please bear in mind that this Hollywood star's sister ship, *Olympic*, completed an illustrious career of twenty-four years before ending up at the breakers.

Mostly forgotten by the popular press was the fact that the builders never claimed she was unsinkable. The words they used were 'practically unsinkable'. There is a difference. But never let the facts get in the way of a good story. Their claim was based on the fact the ship had a double bottom. Unfortunately, the ice sliced into the ship on the side and not the bottom.

After the enormous success of James Cameron's movie *Titanic*, there came moves for two 'practically' unthinkable full-size replicas. First off was the eccentric, but somewhat erratic, Australian billionaire Clive Palmer. For many years he proclaimed to be well advanced with building a seagoing replica. First it was set to be finished in 2012. Then that date was moved to 2018. After gala public relations launches around the world, nothing further was heard.

Not so ambitious were the Chinese, who said they were all set to build a theme park full-sized version. This would most definitely have been an 'it' and not a 'she' as it would never go to sea. Instead, it was designed to sit in a reservoir. Building began in 2016 and, although much hyped, it has yet to eventuate.

Both these copy projects received their fair share of criticism and were labelled as tasteless and guilty of trivialising a horrific tragedy. However, for those with a dissimilar mindset, there are two half-size reproductions in the United States: one in Branson, Missouri, and the other in Pigeon Forge, Tennessee.

Was it the Worst Disaster?

With the loss of an estimated 1,500 lives, *Titanic* is often named as the worst passenger ship disaster in history. Alas, this is far from true. In 1940, the Luftwaffe sank the British Cunard liner RMS *Lancastria* at the cost of an estimated 4,000 lives. Another wartime victim was Cunard's *Lusitania*, which lost 1,198 lives. So, the combined loss of *Titanic* and *Lusitania* is still less than that of *Lancastria*. She holds the unfortunate record of having the biggest loss of any single British ship.

The worst passenger ship disaster of all was the German ship MV *Wilhelm Gustloff*, which lost an estimated 9,000 lives. Her story is in Chapter 8.

Was *Titanic*, which remember was boasted as 'practically unsinkable', faulty in construction? Not by the standards of the day. They were well built by the famous shipyard of Harland & Wolff to be the biggest and most luxurious ships on the Atlantic.

True, the third of the three sisters, *Britannic*, sunk before she even went into passenger service. But there were extenuating circumstances. She was no sooner completed than requisitioned by the British Government to serve as a hospital ship for the First World War. She was sunk by a mine. But there is a bit of difference between hitting a mine in a war zone and hitting an iceberg in a well-known, seasonal field of icebergs.

To my mind, it occurred because Captain Edward Smith succumbed to the public relations pressures to get to New York in record time for the waiting media. To do this, he must have felt it necessary to take a few risks by maintaining speed through an ice-field area. This drive for punctuality could only have been increased by the presence of the chairman of the White Star Line on board.

Captain Smith was an experienced captain and in fact was making his final voyage on the new ship before his retirement. His career had not been without mishaps, but, unlike some others, I am not going to point the accusative finger at him as there are many conflicting stories by survivors of his actions. The simple fact is that I was not there. Thank heavens for that.

However, I do believe the accusations of excessive speed is the reason why Cunard, which was later forced to merge with rival White Star Line, to this day make it very clear the company has no interest in speed for speed's sake.

On this first and final voyage, Captain Smith was off to a bad start. While clearing the berth in a crowded Southampton dock area, the thrust of her propellers created a strong current that snapped the lines of the nearby moored SS *City of New York*. Breaking from the dock, this ship was then sucked in a drift to *Titanic*. The tugs went into emergency action and managed to pull *Titanic* out and push *City of New York* back against the dock. This was done with just 4ft to spare.

A collision would have meant repairs and delays, and that fateful voyage might never have been made at all.

Already running an hour late, *Titanic* presses on to her first scheduled European passenger pick-up port of Cherbourg, France, and then more passengers in Queenstown, Ireland. Still at less than full capacity, she sets off for New York.

The day before the ship sank, Captain Smith curiously cancels the planned passenger lifeboat drill, allegedly wanting to deliver one last Sunday service before going into his retirement.

At the time, God may have been a bit preoccupied elsewhere, but he did arrange other ships to send warnings that there were icebergs ahead.

Captain Smith changes his course a bit further south but did not significantly slow his ship. A little later another ship radios a warning of heavy pack ice and large icebergs, but the wireless operator does not pass this message on to the bridge. The 46,000-ton *Titanic* thunders on through the cold night at a speed of nearly 24mph.

Possible Rescue with Sight

Just before eleven at night, the *Californian*, which is nearby, radios *Titanic*: 'Say, old man, we are stopped and surrounded by ice.' *Titanic*'s radio operator reportedly says, 'Shut up! Shut up! I am busy.' He is handling passengers' private messages to shore.

Wireless was a new feature on ships, and it is probable the operator did not know the significance of the message. His negligence and ignorance of priorities cost him his life.

Just half an hour later, the sole lookout is on watch without binoculars as they have been mislaid. On a moonless night, with his naked eyes, he spots an iceberg directly ahead. He immediately calls the bridge.

Straight away, the order is given to put the helm over, reverse engines and close watertight doors. But it is too late, and the iceberg slides down the ship's hull, rupturing five of the watertight compartments. This brings Captain Smith to the bridge.

The tear in the steel side is 300ft long. Ironically, I think, that if the ship had not swerved and instead met the iceberg head on, there would have been less damage, and if the ship had not reversed away to leave a gaping hole open to the sea, the water could not have flooded in so fast and certainly given considerably more time to abandon ship. But then it's all very well to be wise after the event.

The ship is in calm water and the damage is surveyed. It is estimated *Titanic* has only one or two hours before sinking.

At midnight, the lifeboats are readied for launch. The twenty lifeboats will hold 1,178 people, but there are more than 2,200 on board. Belatedly, the order is given for women and children first.

A radio distress signal is sent and rockets are fired, but the nearest to respond is *Carpathia* from the rival Cunard company. She is 58 nautical miles away but, answering the call of the brotherhood of the sea, she speeds through the icefields to the rescue.

On board *Californian*, less than 10 miles away, the radio operator has gone to bed. However, those on board see rockets and a flashing Morse light. Remarks are also made about the ship's lights being at a sloping angle. Theoretically, the captain could have got his ship to the rescue very quickly and saved many lives if he only had recognised these were all the indications of a sinking ship.

Much has been written about this, but it is a part of the story just too awful to contemplate. All I can offer in *Californian*'s defence is that the radio operator was asleep and rocket signalling was new at the time.

Meanwhile, panic is growing on board *Titanic* as the lifeboats are loaded in a disorderly fashion, with several pulling away from the sinking ship with only a few people on board. In a later interview recorded by the BBC, a young purser, Frank Prentice, goes up on the port side and encourages people into the lifeboats in the traditional order of women and children first.

A young wife says she doesn't want to go without her husband. They are on their honeymoon. The assistant purser tells her not to worry, her husband will be along later. In the meantime, he helps her into her life jacket and sees her lowered away in a half-empty lifeboat.

Other passengers are hanging back, fearful of the 70ft drop, and do not believe the ship is going to sink. Said Prentice, 'The lifeboats could hold 50, and if only they had been filled, we could have saved 800 whereas we only saved 500.'

When the ship gives a sudden steep lurch, all the lifeboats on the upside can no longer be lowered as the angle is too steep. Now everybody wants to get into the boats. With third-class passengers being pushed to the back of the queue, an officer tries to restore a semblance of order by firing his gun three times into the air.

Finally, Frank Prentice finds he cannot help anymore and puts on his life jacket and goes into the freezing water and certain death. But he is lucky, a lifeboat finds him and pulls him from the water into the boat.

But now he has hypothermia, is viciously cold and certain to die. But in the lifeboat is the lady who didn't want to go without her husband. She recognises him and gives up her blanket to warm him.

Said the purser, 'First I saved her life, and then later she saved mine.'

Unfortunately, the lady's husband did not survive.

At 2.20 a.m. *Titanic* plunges to the bottom of the ocean, still 1,300 miles from New York City.

Just over an hour after *Titanic* has sunk, *Carpathia* arrives on the scene and begins taking aboard the surviving passengers who have made it into the lifeboats. Those in the freezing water who had not been pulled quickly into the boats had no chance of surviving long.

When dawn breaks, the terrible scene is fully revealed. *Californian* finally closes the scene. Offering to help, *Carpathia* directs her to make one last sweep for survivors while she hurries back to New York with the sick and wounded.

Carpathia arrives three days later with 705 survivors. Large crowds are gathered at the pier, but rather than the air being filled with the excitement expected for *Titanic*'s arrival, it hangs sodden with rain and the fear of hundreds worrying for their loved ones.

The crowd scans the passengers lining the rails and begins desperately calling out names as they search for their relatives. Few are successful. Of the 2,208 on board *Titanic*, only 705 have survived.

The Unsinkable Molly Brown

The tragedy revealed numerous tales of cowardice, ineptitude and extraordinary bravery. While *Titanic* proved sinkable, one of the first-class passengers, oil heiress Molly Brown, did not. Molly might have been very much an American society lady, but she had grit and determination equalled by few.

Spurning an early lifeboat rescue, she helped many others to get away before finally boarding one herself. The crewman in charge of the lifeboat was anxious to get clear before the boat was sucked under and did not want to pick up anyone from the icy cold water. But Molly could see there was room in the boat for others and threatened to throw the crewman overboard if he did not go back for them.

Once safely on board the rescue ship *Carpathia*, she then set about organising a committee of first-class passengers to help the second- and third-class passengers aboard. There is no doubt this was a first-class lady and she was honoured with a special gold medal award for bravery and, of course, a Broadway musical and a Hollywood film.

Also heroic was the ship's orchestra, consisting of eight musicians, making up both a three-piece and a five-piece ensemble. These two groups gathered on deck to play music to help calm the passengers waiting to be loaded into the lifeboats.

As the ship sunk gently lower and lower into the freezing water, their final tune was reported as the hymn 'Nearer, My God, to Thee'.

All eight musicians died.

There are reports that the captain thanked the musicians, then went up to the wheelhouse and, according to some, shot himself. In those days, for the captain to go down with his ship was an honoured tradition. All in all, it might have been preferable to facing the inevitable boards of inquiry. We will never know the real truth. Captain Smith went down with his ship.

One of the key heroes for saving the lives of those on *Titanic* was Captain Rostron of *Carpathia*. More details are in the biography of *Carpathia* in this book.

Changing Life at Sea

Rearranging the deckchairs on *Titanic* has become a commonly used expression for hopelessly lost causes. The saying was originated by the *Washington Post*'s Rogers Morton, who wrote, 'I'm not going to rearrange the furniture on the deck of the Titanic.'

However, out of death comes renewal and the loss of *Titanic* caused a major rethink in both ship design and better safety procedures at sea.

If you saw the movie, you know all about the ship breaking in two. It was not so dramatic a break as in Cameron's version. The tearing apart of the two halves of *Titanic* most likely occurred after she sank below the waves: a scene possibly a bit tame for a Hollywood blockbuster. But I have no petty quarrels with the film. It certainly made a lasting impression around the world.

To me, one of the most horrific aspects of the tragedy was the attitude of White Star Line. For instance, when the band was signed on, they had to agree to have the cost of their uniforms docked from their wages. The minute the ship went down, the company stopped their pay. And if that wasn't bad enough, White Star then sent bills demanding payment for the lost uniforms to the grieving families. The company also made excessive charges for the retrieved bodies of crew to be returned to their families.

In 2022, a quarter of a century after Cameron's movie, *Norwegian Sun* had a mild collision with a growler iceberg in Alaska. This promptly sent the cruise ship back home to Seattle for repairs.

On the way, whimsical couples lined up on her foredeck to parody a pose for their cell phones of a famous scene in that movie. You guessed it: a windswept Kate Winslet, arms widespread and with Leonardo DiCaprio close behind gripping her waist to stop her flying off *Titanic*'s bow.

Sadly, *Titanic* added five more lives to her death toll in June 2023. A specially designed submersible, carrying passengers to view the wreck of the *Titanic* on the seabed 12,500ft below sea level, failed to surface at the dive site. Prior to the incident, the founder of the submersible company, Stockton Rush, was quoted as saying, 'If you just want to be safe, don't get out of bed.' Mr Rush was on board at the time of the tragedy.

3

RMS *Empress of Ireland*

RMS *Empress of Ireland*. (Library and Archives Canada, PA-116389, via Flickr
CC BY 2.0)

Born	1906
Died	1914
GRT	14,191
Length	570ft
Beam	66ft
Passengers	1,542
Crew	373
Line	Canadian Pacific SS Company
Sister ship	*Empress of Britain*

Death on the St Lawrence

Nowadays, the name Canadian Pacific conjures up mental images of trains chuffing across the Canadian Rockies, but they also rocked ships across the Atlantic and the Pacific. The shipping side of the business operated under the name of Canadian Pacific Steamship Company.

Initially, Canadian Pacific entered the Canada to United Kingdom transatlantic race with the purchase of three ships from Elder Dempster. The company had immediate success and in 1904 decided to build two new identical ships with greater passenger capacity and faster speeds, enabling a voyage from Quebec to Liverpool in less than four days.

When it came to naming, it was first suggested they should be the *Empress of Germany* and *Empress of Austria*. However, it was decided to be more diplomatic and keep it in the Commonwealth. Thus, they became *Empress of Britain* and *Empress of Ireland*.

Both ships had twin screws and two funnels and a service speed of 18 knots. Safety features included eleven watertight compartments and twenty-four watertight doors. It was calculated they could stay afloat even if two adjacent compartments were flooded.

Empress of Ireland was launched in January 1906 and began her maiden voyage six months later. First-class passengers were well catered for: two enclosed promenade decks, a nice luxury for cold conditions, and a grand piano took pride of place in the music room. This was sandwiched between a café forward and a smoking room aft. One deck below was the first-class restaurant with a separate dining room for children. Don't you wish you had one of those at home! For cabins, passengers had a choice of two- and four-berth configurations.

Second class faired reasonably well with much the same amenities but on a smaller and less lavish scale. Now we come to third class. This was designated, in the terms of the times, as being for lower-class travellers and emigrants. It was very crowded, but gave some limited access to the open deck, had two small public rooms, and others for the ladies, smoking, dining and a bar. Accommodation included large, open dormitories consisting of cots mounted two high with long wooden benches.

If you think that sounds tough, imagine how it would feel to be left standing on the dock at Liverpool, surrounded by all your prized possessions, waving your ship goodbye, when you were meant to be on her. That was the fate of nearly 100 migrants who had paid their fare and arrived at the dock to be told there was no more room. They were told to wait for the next ship.

Today, that would be the end of a ship's career there and then, but she sailed for the next eight years between Liverpool and Canada, ending her voyage at Quebec City during the summer months. In winter, when the St Lawrence River was frozen, she terminated at Saint John, New Brunswick. All in all, although travelling through difficult waters, she led a largely uneventful life.

It was the St Lawrence River that was her eventual undoing. She left Quebec City at 4.30 p.m. on 28 May 1914 and made her usual way down the St Lawrence River. It was her ninety-sixth crossing, but it was to be her last.

Empress of Ireland was two-thirds full, carrying 1,057 passengers and 420 crew. Newly appointed Captain Henry Kendall was making his first trip down the St Lawrence River in command. At Pointe-au-Père, just before the river begins to widen out, she stopped to drop off the pilot and pick up mail.

Setting off again in the early hours, the crew glimpsed, a few miles distant, the lights of another ship coming up the St Lawrence River. A fog bank rolled in, quickly obscuring the lights. It was the Norwegian collier SS *Storstad:* a 6,000-ton ship, riding low in the water with a full load of coal and a reinforced icebreaking bow.

Approaching each other in the fog, they took to sounding their whistles to warn each other of their presence. But often, in thick fog, it is hard to determine the exact direction of the deep booming.

Just before 2 a.m., *Storstad* suddenly appeared out of the fog and, before any effective evasive action could be undertaken, crashed right into the middle of *Empress of Ireland*'s starboard side, smashing a huge gaping hole and immediately killing many third-class passengers.

Captain Kendall grabbed a megaphone and yelled at the *Storstad* to keep her engines running forward to stop up the huge hole created and give them time to launch their lifeboats. However, five seconds later, the current in the St Lawrence drifted *Storstad* away and water flooded through the gaping hole in *Empress*'s side. Many of the passengers and crew on the lower decks were drowned immediately. With some of the lower portholes left open, the sea flooded in at such a rate that escape was nearly impossible.

Those on the upper decks made for the lifeboats, but the ship was now listing so badly it became impossible to launch the boats on the port side.

The one attempt made saw the boat hit the side of *Empress* and tip over and send the occupants straight into the icy waters of the St Lawrence. On the starboard side they managed to get five boats away.

Six minutes after the collision, the power on *Empress* failed and five minutes after that the ship rolled onto her starboard side. Passengers scrambled onto the port side but within ten minutes the bow rose briefly out of the water and Canadian Pacific's fastest and most luxurious ship was gone.

Meanwhile *Storstad*, with its reinforced bow, was floating safely and quickly launched her lifeboats to rescue the survivors. *Empress* had managed to send a radio distress message and the first rescue boat arrived at 3.10 a.m.

With hundreds of people in the near-freezing water, quick rescue was essential to prevent hypothermia and drowning. Unfortunately, 1,012 people lost their lives.

While there was a dispute as to whether the captain ordered the watertight doors to be closed, the fact remains that divers later found them mostly open. The problem was that they could only be closed manually, unlike on *Titanic* where all they had to do was hit an electrical switch on the bridge.

However, *Empress of Ireland* did benefit from the *Titanic* disaster. To conform with new maritime regulations introduced in the aftermath of *Titanic*'s sinking, her wooden lifeboats were replaced with sixteen steel-hulled lifeboats. There were also another twenty-six collapsible lifeboats. This gave her a total lifeboat capacity of 1,686. That was 280 people more than the ship carried.

Always Travel First Class

While early newspaper reports speculated on the number of souls lost, the full facts came out at the official inquiry. The total number of people on board was announced as 1,477, of whom 31.5 per cent survived. It appears that out of the eighty-seven first-class passengers, 41 per cent survived. Second class came off second best, with only 19 per cent of the 253 on board surviving.

Now we come to the lower decks of the third-class passengers packed in below the ship's waterline. Of the 717 third-class passengers, only 18 per cent survived.

Also on board were 167 members of the Salvation Army travelling to London with their families. Only eight of them were saved.

Not surprisingly, the crew came off best of all. This is because they were first on the upper decks to launch lifeboats and knew their way around the ship and the sea.

One of the last ones away was Captain Kendall, but even then, it was not a decision of his making. He was on the bridge leaning out and barking orders when the ship lurched on her side and catapulted him into the water. The ship was going down and taking him with her but he managed to surface and grasp onto a piece of floating wooden grating.

Picked up by a nearby lifeboat, he quickly took command, directing the crew to find survivors and take them to *Storstad* for safety. He then guided the lifeboat back and forth until no one was left who hadn't drowned or been claimed by hypothermia.

As soon as he boarded *Storstad* he was reported as storming to the bridge and yelling to Captain Andersen, 'You have sunk my ship!'

The Blame Game

An eleven-day case was brought in Quebec before a commission of inquiry headed by Lord Mersey. He was no stranger to maritime disasters as he had presided over both the *Titanic* and *Lusitania* inquiries. In that respect, his CV was looking pretty good!

It appears that both ships changed course while in the fog bank. First it was *Empress of Ireland* assuming the fastest course to Liverpool and secondly *Storstad* responding to a change in *Empress*'s navigation lights to pass port side light to port side light. *Empress* was planning to pass starboard side light to starboard side light. This shows they were attempting to follow the old sailor's maxim of:

When all three lights I see ahead, I turn to starboard and show my red. Green to green, red to red, perfect safety, go ahead. But if to starboard red appear, it is my duty to keep clear. To act as judgement says is proper, turn to starboard, back or stop her. And, if upon my port is seen, a steamer's starboard light of green. I hold my course and watch to see, that green to port keeps clear of me. Both in safety and in doubt, always keep a good look out. In danger with no room to turn, ease her, stop her, go astern.

That's all very well in the classroom, but in a thick fog bank when you can't see the lights all the time and you don't have the benefit of modern navigational aids, it's not so simple.

However, *Storstad* was deemed at fault for changing her course to starboard, thus causing the collision. The chief officer was in command at the time, and he was also criticised for not rousing his captain in good time to deal with a developing situation in thick fog. It was also insinuated that, to keep her schedule, *Empress* was travelling too fast for the conditions.

Storstad was given to Canadian Pacific in compensation but went on to meet her own fate in the First World War by being sunk by a German U-boat.

The disaster also led to a rethink of ship bow design. Ships commonly had bows that were nearly straight up and down and could even be slightly forward at the water line. In the event of a collision, the initial impact is thus taken at or below the water line and thus inflicts maximum damage.

Reversing the sheer to have the top of the bow forward of the waterline makes the ship less of a battering ram. It certainly looks better.

Today, however, many ships have a projecting bulbous bow at the waterline that acts as a wave breaker and reduces slamming into the seas. However, modern navigational aids ensure those on the bridge can tell which other ships are in the vicinity and their direction of travel.

Empress of Ireland sank to the bottom in only 130ft of water and the funnels were still visible just beneath the surface. A salvage crew was able to recover 318 bags of mail and 212 bars of silver bullion. Due to the strong currents, one professional diver lost his life in the process. The low depth also attracted amateur divers and this has resulted in the loss of another six lives.

Monuments were erected on the nearby shore, while the Salvation Army has a special monument at Toronto's Mount Pleasant Cemetery and holds a memorial service there every year. The inscription reads: 'In Sacred Memory of 167 Officers and Soldiers of the Salvation Army Promoted to Glory from the *Empress of Ireland* at Daybreak, Friday, May 29, 1914.'

4

RMS *Lusitania*

RMS *Lusitania* coming into port, possibly in New York, 1907–13. (George Grantham Bain, Library of Congress cph.3g13287, via WikimediaCommons)

Born	1907
Died	1915
GRT	31,550
Length	787ft
Beam	87ft
Passengers	2,198
Crew	850
Line	Cunard Line
Sister ship	*Mauretania**

* The first RMS *Mauretania*, born in 1906. The second RMS *Mauretania* was born in 1939. You can read more about her in Chapter 12.

Civilian Ship Torpedoed

Long before the First World War, Britain and Germany were battling it out on the Atlantic to have the largest, fastest and most luxurious liners. Since 1897, the Germans had held the Blue Riband, the record for the fastest Atlantic crossing, and Britain was determined to get it back with the introduction of two new liners, *Lusitania* and *Mauretania*.

The British Government advanced Cunard a loan of £2.6 million for their building on the basis that additional payments would be made if the two ships were capable of being armed and the government could requisition them in the event of war. Both the ships were fitted with turbine engines rather than the standard reciprocating engines then in service and they did the trick. The coveted Blue Riband was theirs.

Lusitania, named after a Roman province that covered a portion of modern-day Portugal, was the first of the duo in service. The ship was not only the biggest but was also palatial in style. Even steerage open accommodation was spurned, with all third-class passengers accommodated in four- or six-berth cabins.

Two Sides to Every Issue

An interesting aspect of the ship's design was that its coal bunkers ran along the sides of the boiler rooms. This gave added protection to the engines in the event of enemy action. She was also designed to carry twelve rapid-fire 6in guns, making her into an armed merchant ship.

This was bound to make the Germans take notice. Indeed, the ship played an important role in fuelling an arms race in the lead-up to the First World War.

After the outbreak, in January 1915, *Lusitania* hoisted the Stars and Stripes of the neutral USA to fool German warships into not sinking her by sailing under false colours. All is fair in love and war, but this was certainly not cricket and the Germans quickly came to learn of this deception by reading the press.

Jingoism and patriotism aside, given all this, it is easy to understand why the German Embassy in Washington DC sent warnings to New York newspapers to the effect that the passengers travelling on Allied ships did so at their own risk. When it came to the sailing of the *Lusitania* from pier 54 in

New York on 1 May 1915, the Germans gave fair and prominent display warnings in the press that the ship was known to be carrying munitions and passengers should not sail on her as she would be sunk.

Most passengers ignored the warnings. Surely, it was just posturing?

At the last minute, preparing to cross the Atlantic, how likely are you to abort and change your travel plans immediately? As we have seen with Covid-19, passengers are prepared to risk all to keep to their planned travel activities. And why would the Germans fire on a civilian ship full of American civilians and take the risk of bringing the United States into the war?

They Did It

So, on the first day of May 1915, 1,692 souls embarked on a voyage to hell. As she neared the U-boat lanes near the Irish coast, *Lusitania*'s crew closed the watertight doors and swung the lifeboats out as precautionary measures. Her captain also doubled the number of lookouts and kept steam pressure high for emergency full speed.

Remembering the issue of the false flag, if you were a U-boat commander seeing, just after lunch, an enemy ship pop up in your periscope off the coast of Ireland, and knowing warnings had been made and she was armed and carrying enemy munitions, what would you do?

Well, that captain decided to fire one torpedo. It was bang on target and struck *Lusitania*. A few seconds later, without firing a second torpedo, there was another explosion inside the ship. She immediately took on a heavy list to starboard and sank bow first in under twenty minutes.

After the war it was revealed she was heavily laden with munitions, including more than 4 million rounds of machine-gun ammunition. Did the Germans sink her, or was such a sudden sinking caused by the torpedo detonating the cargo carried in her own holds?

The ship took 1,201 men, women and children with her. Of these, 123 were Americans. It has been claimed this is what brought the United States into the war. If that was the case, it took two years to do so.

Bodies were washing up on the coast just 10 miles away for the next three weeks. Only 761 people survived.

5

RMS *Carpathia*

RMS *Carpathia*.

Born	1903
Died	1918
GRT	13,555
Length	558ft
Beam	64ft
Passengers	2,550
Crew	166
Line	Cunard Line
Sister ships	*Ivernia* and *Saxonia*

Mission of *Titanic* Mercy

At the turn of the twentieth century, the competition to take passengers from the old world to the new was intensifying. Cunard's long hold on the market was beginning to slip. It was not only facing stiff opposition from fellow British company White Star, but also from North German Lloyd and Hamburg America Line.

The company was losing market share and decided to build three new ships with a different approach. These would not compete with the speed and luxury of their rivals but put more emphasis on practicality and run more economically with lower fuel consumption. They also crammed more passengers into a smaller space and thus could offer lower fares. Initially, there was no first class. The target market was a mix of tourists and emigrants. Think of it as an early Butlin's holiday camp at sea.

All three ships were similar in appearance. Each had a single, but very tall, funnel. This was to enable the black smoke and soot from the stack to clear the decks and save passengers from gasping and choking on their morning walk. It made them look a bit odd, but it was preferable to going for the sleeker, swept-back style to make ships look good. Nowadays, Cunard has gone with wind scoop designs, which as well as looking good are very effective. And of course, today's ships are no longer burning coal or dirty diesel.

Adding to the unusual appearance of Cunard's new trio were four tall derricks along the length of the vessels. These gave the ships more of a cargo vessel appearance, but it did enable fast and efficient cargo handling.

First of the threesome was *Ivernia* in 1899, then came *Saxonia* a year later and lastly *Carpathia* in 1902. Only one was to survive the war before being scrapped in 1926.

Slow and Steady

Although originally offering only second- and third-class accommodation, *Carpathia* had a modern approach to comfort with the use of rich upholstery and mahogany furniture. The second-class area included a walnut-panelled smoking room and a handsome library. Third class was spacious for the times, but accommodation was predominantly dormitory style. The dining room was furnished with walls of polished oak and teak and, stretching across the full beam of the ship, could accommodate 300 passengers. There was another smoking room and an area just for the ladies. Heating and cooling fans were installed around the ship.

This design was a successful approach, proving slow and steady wins the tourist and emigrant race. The three ships gave a boost to profitability, which the company used to help finance the construction of new fleet leaders: *Lusitania* and *Mauretania*. These bigger and faster ships enabled Cunard to again compete in the luxury end of the market. Perhaps another example of using the poor to improve the lives of the rich, but it would be fairer to say Cunard was catering to all passengers.

Carpathia went quietly about her business, first running from Liverpool to New York, then moving a year later to a run from New York to Croatia's Fiume, now to be found on the map under the name Rijeka. It was an all-stops tour: she voyaged via Gibraltar, Liverpool, Genoa, Naples and Trieste. After the introduction of first class, she carried everyone from the rich to poorer Hungarian emigrants.

With the conversion completed, she could now carry 2,500 passengers. Remember, this was a small 13,555-ton ship and she was carrying about the same number of passengers as cruise ships five times her size do today. There was no room to swing a cat, although I hasten to add that the cat-o'-nine tails was not a feature on Cunard ships. There was also a definite dearth of movie theatres, dodgem car rides, casinos, skating rings, wave riders and health and well-being centres.

Come to think of it, I would have really liked *Carpathia*.

Moulding a Captain

Although a fine ship, she had none of the fame, glamour and glory of the big, fast liners. She lived in their shadows but in 1912 she suddenly burst onto the world's stage. This was due to the appointment of a very special captain.

Arthur Rostron was a nautical 'lifer', a first-class seaman through and through. He left his Lancashire school at the age of 13 to continue a specialist maritime education with the famous HMAS *Conway* school training ship. After twenty-seven years of working his way through the ranks, in 1912, at the age of 43, he was appointed captain of *Carpathia*.

This was a man to be admired and respected. He wasn't the sort of chap you could clap on the shoulder and suggest nipping to the local for a pint.

He was religious, a disciplinarian who ran a very tight ship but was deeply respected by his crew. He was articulate, fast thinking, upright and a well-spoken gentleman proud of the uniform he wore.

In later years, as captain of *Mauretania*, his dedication to strict order and always departing exactly on schedule resulted in the crew nicknaming the ship the 'Rostron Express'. He helped build the precedent for Cunard captains to be renowned for their seafaring skills and their dedicated professionalism.

None could have put it better about the moulding of Cunard captains than the writer Mark Twain. He was no stranger to ships as he adopted his pen name while travelling as a passenger on a Mississippi steamboat. He heard the seaman swinging the lead to measure the depth of water under the ship and often calling out, 'By the mark, twain'. This meant the lead-weighted line had sunk to the second mark on the rope, indicating there was two fathoms of safe water under the vessel.

Captain Rostron, only three months into his spell as master of *Carpathia*, was resting in his cabin just by the bridge. They were four days out of New York when, just after midnight, his radio and first officer suddenly burst in on him. He said his first thought was, 'Who the dickens is this cheeky beggar coming into my cabin without knocking.'

Excitedly, they announced *Titanic* had broadcast a distress signal. Rostron immediately swung into action, demonstrating his extreme professionalism.

He quickly issued a stream of commands, first ordering three lookouts, instead of just one as on *Titanic*, and the engine telegraph set to full steam ahead. Extra stokers were roused from their beds to help fire up the boilers to maximum and the heating to passenger quarters was switched off to divert all available power to the engines. The little *Carpathia*, normally running at about 14 knots, picked up speed to steam at nearly 18 knots.

The estimated time to reach *Titanic* was four hours. During this period, the lifeboats were prepared and swung out ready for launching. The three ship's doctors were directed to prepare the ship's dining rooms with the needed medical supplies to treat the wounded and sick. Crew were detailed to help the survivors to the treatment areas and to take their names for a register of survivors.

The chief steward was ordered to make sure coffee and refreshments could be offered promptly. Preparations were made to make officer accommodation, including the captain's, readied for the rescued. Third-class dormitories were rearranged to clear a dormitory for survivor use.

Stewards were placed in the alleyways to reassure *Carpathia*'s own passengers they were perfectly secure but to tell them to please remain in their own cabins. A chair swing was placed at each gangway to raise the sick and wounded, while ladders and scrambling nets were hung over the sides.

In total, Captain Rostron issued twenty-three orders and prepared *Carpathia*, without any noise or confusion, to make the most efficient rescue possible. Meanwhile, *Californian* was hove-to in the ice field and within sight of *Titanic*, but slept on.

Carpathia arrived at 3.45 a.m. *Titanic* had gone and the only thing to be seen were her laden lifeboats. Skilfully, *Carpathia* avoided the ice to retrieve the occupants and, where possible, the boats as well. Asked about the risks of his speeding through the icebergs at night, the religious Captain Rostron said, 'A hand other than mine was on the wheel that night.'

In recognition of his remarkable seamanship, he received a commemorative cup and a gold medal. In 2015, that cup was sold at auction for US$200,000. Other awards included the US Cross of Honor, a medal from the Liverpool Shipwreck and Humane Society, a gold medal from the Shipwreck Society of New York, an OBE from the British Government and finally a knighthood.

There is more on *Carpathia*'s role in the *Titanic* disaster in Chapter 2.

The War Years

Now a famous ship, *Carpathia* went on to even more excitement. Sadly, this brought her to a terrible end. When the First World War broke, she was requisitioned as a troopship and painted in battleship grey, including her proud, tall, red funnel.

For the next four years, *Carpathia* carried US and Canadian troops to the European battle grounds. Her final voyage came towards the end of the war. In 1918, when off the coast of Ireland, she was travelling as part of a convoy, zigzagging from Liverpool to Boston. Zigzagging did not prevent a German submarine U-boat sinking the lead ship. *Carpathia* was then appointed to lead the convoy.

Three and a half hours later, a torpedo struck *Carpathia*'s engine room, killing five of the crew. She was disabled and now a sitting duck. The second torpedo finished her. The surviving 218 launched the lifeboats and threw over the side all confidential papers, making sure nothing of value could fall into enemy hands. Meanwhile, as per standing orders, the rest of the convoy steamed away as fast as they could.

The age of chivalry was not yet dead. The assassins were gentlemen. Once the lifeboats were loaded and pulled away, the U-boat fired a third torpedo to sink *Carpathia*.

It was not the last we were to hear of *Carpathia*. In 2000, the National Underwater Marine Agency, founded by US author Clive Cussler, discovered her sitting upright on the seabed at a depth of 514ft.

The rights to the wreck were purchased by Premier Exhibitions, an American company managing relics from *Titanic*. A 2007 expedition retrieved artefacts from *Carpathia*.

In a 2016 auction, a first-class soup plate and a salvaged porthole were reported sold for US$900 each and a navigational sextant used during the rescue went for $89,800. Among the more unusual collectibles were single pieces of coal recovered from the boiler room. Bidding started at $25 apiece.

Some are still available. The way energy prices are heading, you can be forgiven for thinking it might soon prove quite a bargain.

6

SS *Morro Castle*

SS *Morro Castle*.

Born	1930
Died	1934
GRT	11,520
Length	508ft
Beam	71ft
Passengers	489
Crew	240
Line	Ward Line
Sister ship	SS *Oriente*

The Ship that Beat Prohibition

The jitterbug, the Charleston and the shimmy are playing in the dance halls. There is no television: those at home are listening to the radio, playing checkers, charades or the popular new game of Monopoly, where you can snap up imaginary properties at the throw of a dice. What better time to introduce a money game than during the world's worst recession?

This is the Great Depression. Workers are lining up at soup kitchens as they suffer job loss and income reduction. These are the days of the underground speakeasies, running the risk of a five-year jail term for selling liquor. There is nowhere to legally have a drink. Unless you take a cruise.

This was not the sole reason why Ward Line decided to build two new ships for the New York to Havana run, but it helped. Even more encouraging was the US Congress offering to subsidise as much as 75 per cent of new ship construction and allowing up to twenty years to repay it. Together, these offerings were too good to resist, and Ward Line succumbed.

First off Virginia's Newport News Shipbuilding slipway was *Morro Castle*, a luxuriously furnished two-class ship, with a top speed of 20 knots. On her 1930 maiden voyage, she completed the 1,100-mile southbound voyage to Havana in just under fifty-nine hours. Coming back, she shaved another hour off the journey. So, for her day, she was fast.

Despite the poor economic scene, with good value rates she proved very popular and succeeded in maintaining strong passenger lists. But she only had four years of cruising before tragedy struck in September 1934.

Morro Castle was on the way back from Havana when she encountered strong winds and driving rain. This is certainly not unusual on this route and passengers retreated to their cabins. Even the captain opted for his meal to be delivered to his quarters. But his problem was not seasickness. He was complaining of stomach ache and a short time later he died while on the bridge. The shipping company said he had a heart attack, but others claimed he was poisoned by a discontented crew member.

Command to finish the journey was thrust onto his chief officer. Passengers were informed of the captain's death and were assured they were in capable hands, although some of the crew were harbouring doubts.

Fire at Sea

A few hours into his command, the new captain faced increasingly stormy conditions. Just before three in the morning, while she was off Long Beach Island, a fire was discovered in a first-class writing room locker. The cabinet was used to store blankets, which, as was usual in those days, had been cleaned with flammable dry-cleaning liquid. On its own, that might not have caused a major problem, but, in the ship's construction, no considera-tion had been given to using flame-proof panelling and furniture. Within twenty minutes, the flames gained a firm hold.

The ship had five fire doors, but the automatic trip mechanism was not on. Even so, it is doubtful the fire doors would have been much use as there was a 6in opening at the top that would allow the flames to lick through.

The fire spread rapidly and was soon sweeping from bow to stern. The new captain had not varied her heading and kept at speed, aiming into the wind, enflaming the fire even more and sweeping it along the length of the ship. His intention was to beach her on the Jersey shore. However, as the fire intensified, it took out the steerage system and eventually all engine power failed. Some crew broke windows on several decks in attempts to reach passengers, but again, this only allowed the wind to enter the ship and intensify the fire.

There was a large degree of panic. Passengers had not been required to attend a fire drill and now it seemed many of the crew were only interested in saving themselves. The first lifeboats away were mainly filled with crew. Passengers claimed they didn't even try to pick up people who had lowered themselves into the water. As there were few crew left to operate the life-boats, half of the boats were not even launched.

The radio officer claimed the order to transmit a Mayday call only came shortly before the electrical power was cut. Due to the conditions, rescue ships were slow to respond and the size of the waves made it hard to find people in the water.

On board, mayhem reigned. With no generator power, the ship was in darkness and passengers found it hard to find a safe way to the aft open deck, while most of the crew fled to the foredeck.

In the absence of any deck officers, cruise director Bob Smith bravely stepped in to try and bring some order. Years later, I was to sail with Bob as a fellow crew member when he was cruise director of *Nieuw Amsterdam*. Of course, I tried to get him to give me the inside story of what happened.

But Bob just shook his head and said it was the past and we should not dwell on it. He certainly gave me the impression it was something he didn't want to relive.

So, I must rely on the reports of surviving passengers. It appears Bob was a hero and tried to stop the panic reigning on board, while running down the corridors, banging on doors to wake passengers and urging them to grab their life jackets and make for the open decks.

He herded them aft and tried to secure life jackets for those without them. He even gave away his own. Bob was one of the last to leave and jumped. He was a former lifeguard and strong swimmer. In the sea, he joined with an assistant purser. They clung together until the purser's white cap caught the eye of a rescue boat and pulled them from the water.

At the resulting inquiry into the loss of 135 lives out of the 540 on board, Bob, maybe a little reluctantly, admitted to having previously made representations to both the captain and the owners about the lack of common safety standards. Furthermore, he had suspicions about the cause of the fire, and considered the new acting captain, Chief Officer Warms, to be 'not determined enough to take command. And maybe he was overcome, confused by the happenings.'

Although Bob was praised by the resulting inquiry, it concluded, in the main, that the efforts made by the crew were lacking in efforts to go to their assigned fire stations, and in assisting in directing passengers to safety.

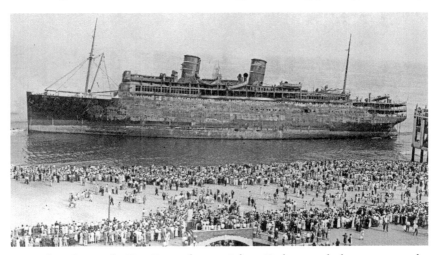

Crowds gather on the New Jersey shore at Asbury Park to see the burnt-out wreck of SS *Morro Castle*.

The rescue efforts also came under examination. The two Coast Guard vessels positioned themselves too far away and were of little practical use. SS *President Cleveland* launched a lifeboat to motor around *Morro Castle*, but in the high waves reported they could not spot anyone in the water. She immediately retrieved her boat and sailed off.

The full seriousness of the situation did not appear to be recognised until radio stations began breaking into their broadcasts with reports of bodies washing up on the New Jersey shore. This was what brought rescuers rushing to the scene.

They were eventually joined by *Morro Castle* herself, drifting onto the shore at Asbury Park. Here, the fires smouldered on for another two days. *Morro Castle* proved an object of endless fascination to the locals, who were able to wade out and touch her hull with their hands.

She was finally towed away to be sold as scrap. In her wake, she left 135 dead and a vow to build future ships with less flammable materials.

Bob Smith was certainly not put off the seagoing life by the tragedy. Within a few months, he was cruise director of *Queen of Bermuda*. Stories of his hero status followed him throughout his continuing life as a cruise director.

7

SS *Normandie*

SS *Normandie*. (© Courtesy of James A. Flood, from an original colour painting)

Born	1935
Died	1942
GRT	83,423
Length	1,029ft
Beam	118ft
Passengers	1,972
Crew	1,345
Line	French Line

Fairest of Them All

A huge crowd of 50,000 people turned up in Le Havre to see off *Normandie* on her maiden voyage in May 1935. She was big, she was bold, she was beautiful. Four days, three hours and two minutes later, she reached New York, thus seizing the coveted Blue Riband for the fastest crossing from Italy's liner *Rex*.

Although generally billed as the most glamorous liner ever built, it is a claim that can be challenged. I must confess to being a loyal fan of *Queen Mary* and thus possibly a trifle biased. For argumentative purposes I could also offer the Dutch liner *Nieuw Amsterdam* and Italy's *Leonardi De Vinci* as worthy but much smaller contenders. However, based on the published pictures and books, the consensus among the greater liner fan community is that *Normandie* is the true holder of this accolade.

Even Stephen Payne, designer of *Queen Mary 2*, concedes his design was very much influenced by *Normandie*. But Stephen was restricted by today's commercial reality calling for more and more cabins with balconies and thus meaning many more cabins piled up right to the bow.

So it is most unlikely we will ever see another liner built with the graceful sweeping curvature of *Normandie*, with her three proud and dominant three funnels, which, if possibly a little squat, still showed both speed and grace. Which only makes it more tragic that this pride of France, in all her magic majesty and prime as the biggest, grandest and fastest ship on the Atlantic was ruthlessly destroyed by incompetence and possible deliberate wartime sabotage while in the safety of New York Harbor's famed Liner Row.

They say her claim to beauty was unrivalled when it came to her arts décoratifs interior. Sure, it was, but only in first class. That area got all the over-egged trimmings and took up a disproportionate amount of the ship. Second and third class were crammed into much humbler conditions. So although it was very grand for the likes of the wife of French President Albert Lebrun, Irving Berlin, Fred Astaire, Marlene Dietrich, Walt Disney, Douglas Fairbanks, James Stewart and the very British Noël Coward, she won considerably less favour with lesser mortals.

For this reason, the arrival of *Queen Mary* with her superior cabin- and tourist-class accommodations saw *Normandie* lose many of her ordinary passengers. *Queen Mary* also deprived her of the title of the being the biggest ship in the world and the holder of the Blue Riband.

While they competed for the speed title over various crossings, the French fixed the size issue by cleverly enclosing some space on the open decks and making it into a tourist lounge, thus making her bigger than the *Queen Mary* by 2,000 tons. However, *Queen Elizabeth* fixed all this nonsense when she was launched in 1939 by being bigger than both.

In another clash with the British, in 1936 a Royal Air Force plane on torpedo-dropping practice, decided to buzz *Normandie* while she was anchored off Ryde Pier and offloading a British MP's car onto a barge. The plane went so low it clipped the derrick and crashed onto *Normandie*'s bow. There it had to stay until it could be taken off in Le Havre. The pilot survived, only to be court-martialled.

In spite of all her fame and glory, *Normandie* was losing money and the owners had to keep going to the French Government to get financial aid. The outbreak of war saw *Normandie* take refuge in New York, where she remained with French crew members on board. Amidst rumours of possible sabotage, in May 1940, 150 United States Coast Guard (USCG) agents boarded *Normandie* at Manhattan's Pier 88 to defend it against any attack.

Five days after the attack on Pearl Harbor, and with a Vichy government in France, on 12 December 1941, the USCG removed the French crew, took possession of *Normandie* and renamed her USS *Lafayette*.

It was first thought to convert her to an aircraft carrier, but this was dropped in favour of making her into a troopship. A big job, but why did they think it was a good idea to stop the regular fire patrols before conversion started?

Under pressure from Washington, the work sped ahead. However, on 9 February 1942, sparks from a welding torch set fire to life vests filled with kapok and the fire quickly spread. With the latest fire-protection system installed, how did the whole liner catch ablaze? Well, the sickening answer is the internal water-pumping system had been switched off.

The workers gathered to fight the blaze but by the time the fire department arrived fifteen minutes later, the fire had spread and was being fanned by a strong wind blowing it along the length of the ship. The firefighters began pouring 6,000 tons of water onto the blaze. This, of course, caused the ship to begin to list. Then the unforgivable happened. The ship's designer, Vladimir Yourkevitch, arrived and began frantically pleading for the ship's seacocks to be opened to let the ship sink to the seabed. Then she would stay upright and they could pour on as much water as they liked, as long as it was allowed to sink to the bottom of the ship. He insisted that if the firefighters kept doing what they were doing the ship would capsize. His obvious, common-sense suggestions and pleadings were ignored. Thus at 2.45 a.m., at the dock, the *Lafayette* capsized.

Plans to salvage her for future use proved uneconomic. At the end of the war, *Lafayette* was sold for scrap. She never did sail under the US flag.

8

MV *Wilhelm Gustloff*

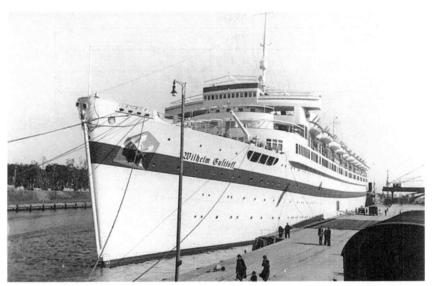

MV *Wilhelm Gustloff* in Danzig. (Bundesarchiv, Bild 183-H27992/Sönnke, Hans/ CC-BY-SA 3.0, via WikimediaCommons)

Born	1938
Died	1945
GRT	25,484
Length	684ft
Beam	77ft
Passengers	1,465
Crew	417
Line	Kriegsmarine

Disaster for Hitler's Cruise Ship

If ever the pub trivia question comes up asking which was the worst passenger shipping disaster, don't say *Titanic*. It most definitely wasn't. The right answer is *Wilhelm Gustloff*.

What's that you say? Never heard of it! Well let's fix that because it is the most fascinating story.

She was constructed as a cruise ship, but one with a difference. Passenger fares were heavily subsidised, and it was more by invitation only. Her name was to be *Adolf Hitler*, but instead, before the launch, it was changed to *Wilhelm Gustloff*, the founder and leader of the Swiss branch of the Nazi Party.

Who would dare make such a decision? Well, none other than Hitler himself. After Wilhelm Gustloff was assassinated in 1936, Hitler was seated next to Gustloff's widow at the funeral, which was also attended by Goebbels, Himmler, Bormann and von Ribbentrop. Was the name change a decision made in a rare compassionate moment? I believe it was a propaganda move to bolster the Swiss Nazi Party. If only the assassin had been able to strike again at that funeral, think how different the world would have been.

The assailant was David Frankfurter, a Jewish student from what is now Croatia. He immediately gave himself up to Swiss police – probably didn't fancy being caught by the SS – and was sentenced to eighteen years in prison, but was pardoned shortly after the war. He should have been given a medal.

The ship was, of course, built in Germany and was one of the world's first purpose-built cruise ships. The lucky owner was the KdF, which roughly translates to 'Strength Through Joy'. This was a national labour initiative set up in 1933 as a tool to promote the advantages of Nazism to the German people and the world. Its departments included the Beauty of Labour for Better Workplaces, the Leisure Time Office for Folklore and Homeland, and the Office for Travel, Hiking, and Holidays.

It was this last department, along with other ships, that operated the *Wilhelm Gustloff*. In 1938, the department booked 10.3 million holidays and became the world's biggest tourism operator.

The goal was to do away with social-class distinctions and ensure all Germans could own cars and take cruises. How did the Nazi Government pay for all this? By a tax on the workers' pay packets of course.

On her third cruise from Hamburg, in the middle of a fierce storm, *Wilhelm Gustloff* came to the rescue of the English coal freighter *Pegaway* in the North Sea. Huge waves had washed onto *Pegaway*'s decks and the ship was taking in water. This caused steering problems and she was starting to sink.

Answering an SOS call, *Wilhelm Gustloff* managed to get a lifeboat away in the huge seas and get close to *Pegaway*. The nineteen crew jumped into the sea, where they were pulled into the lifeboat and saved.

It was good seamanship and good publicity for Hitler. Her next move also had political ramifications. Germany wanted to unify with Austria, and this needed a plebiscite from the citizens of both countries.

Wilhelm Gustloff, as a floating piece of Germany, anchored 5.6 miles offshore from London's Tilbury, just in international waters. She now served as a polling station for German and Austrian citizens living in England. Some 1,172 Germans and 806 Austrians were ferried to the ship to cast their vote. Only ten people voted against it. They probably had to swim back.

Before the Second World War, she made sixty goodwill cruises around Europe and carried 80,000 passengers. With the advent of the war in 1938, she was converted into a hospital ship for the first two years. After the Allies blockaded the German coastline, she was moved to the occupied Polish harbour of Gdynia, where she sat at the dock for four years serving as a barracks for U-boat trainees.

With the tide of the war turning, it became necessary to flee from the advancing Russian Red Army. A naval evacuation named Operation Hannibal was launched and *Wilhelm Gustloff* helped transport civilians and military personnel from Poland and the Baltic States to safety.

The ship left Gdynia at lunchtime on 30 January 1945. On board were an estimated 10,600 people: 8,956 civilians along with 1,644 Gestapo and Nazi officials and their families.

She was sailing as part of a convoy, but engine problems on another of the ships caused the convoy to split up. *Wilhelm Gustloff* was forced to proceed on with just one torpedo boat as escort.

The Baltic is a harsh sea in January. On this particularly cold day the air temperature was in the range of 0–14°F and the sea was thick with ice flows. The low temperatures froze over both the escort's submarine detective capabilities and her anti-aircraft guns.

On the bridge of *Wilhelm Gustloff* was the unusual situation of four captains: the ship's own captain, two merchant marine captains and a U-boat captain. A vigorous discussion was held.

The German submarine captain, fearful of a submarine attack, argued for the use of a close-to-shore course, but the ship's captain, fearful of mines, opted to head for deeper water known to have been cleared. Mistake.

Informed of an oncoming German minesweeper convoy, the captain, concerned about the possibility of a possible collision in the dark, switched on his ship's red and green navigation lights. Another mistake.

Lying in wait was a Soviet submarine. The captain had an alcohol problem and, while he and his crew were off duty, had been caught in a brothel. Not a good look in the Soviet marine. He was facing a court martial.

Possible salvation popped up in his periscope with the sight of *Wilhelm Gustloff*, lit up for all to see. Salivating, the captain followed the ships on their starboard side for two hours. Finally, he surfaced in the dark and then swept around *Wilhelm Gustloff*'s stern, to attack from the side closest to the shore.

The Russians believed in nicknaming their weapons. The first torpedo was named 'For the Motherland', the second 'For Leningrad' and the third 'For the Soviet People'. The fourth, 'For Stalin', was a total failure and jammed in the torpedo tubes.

'For the Motherland' struck the ship's bow, where duty crew members were sleeping. 'Leningrad' hit the accommodation for the women's naval auxiliary, and 'For the Soviet People' hit the engine room, disabling all power and communications.

On board the horribly overcrowded *Wilhelm Gustloff*, due to the discomfort, many passengers had disobeyed orders and taken off their life jackets. The first deaths were caused by a mad, panic-stricken dash to the upper decks, while others were killed immediately in the explosions or drowned by the water flooding into the ship.

On deck, passengers found many lifeboats frozen into their davits and it is believed only nine lifeboats were got away. A sudden steep list of the ship meant that the boats on the high side could not be lowered due to the tilted angle of the ship.

Jumping into the icy Baltic was almost certain death and it is a miracle that any could be saved. German boats, rushing to the scene, managed to rescue 1,252 of the estimated 10,600 on board. Fifty minutes after the torpedoes had been fired, *Wilhelm Gustloff* vanished bow first below the waves.

This was a real blow to Germany, but because of his earlier misdemeanours, the Russian submarine captain was deemed not suitable for the award of Hero of the Soviet Union. He was also downgraded in rank to lieutenant and dishonourably discharged.

Fifteen years later, in 1960, he was reinstated as captain and given a full pension. Forgiveness takes a long time in the Soviet Union, but in 1990, Mikhail Gorbachev finally made him a Hero of the Soviet Union. It was a bit late. By then he was dead.

Along with the largest loss of life resulting from the sinking of a single vessel in history, some believe the ship was also carrying very valuable stolen works of art seized in the countries Germany occupied. Eyewitnesses claimed to have seen the decorative panels of the Amber Room being packaged up and placed aboard *Wilhelm Gustloff*. This was a priceless collection of amber panels backed with gold leaf and mirrors that lined a room in the Catherine Palace, near St Petersburg.

Although diving within 1,600ft of the wreck was prohibited, there have been numerous dives on it. Maybe, the missing treasure is still on *Wilhelm Gustloff*, or it has been magicked away by treasure hunters. Either way, the amber panels have never surfaced.

9

SS *Eastland*

(Later USS *Wilmette*)

SS *Eastland*. (Library of Congress Prints and Photographs Division Washington, D.C. 20540, via WikimediaCommons)

Born	1903
Died	1946
GRT	1,218
Length	265ft
Beam	38ft
Passengers	2,752
Line	Michigan Transportation RMSA Company

Mutiny and Sunk at the Docks

With a loss of 848 lives, the sinking of Chicago's *Eastland* is among the world's worst marine disasters. It cost many more lives than died in the Great Chicago Fire. Worse still, she hadn't even left the dock.

Some blame the sinking on *Titanic*, as new maritime regulations demanded all ships increase their number of lifeboats. On *Eastland*, this meant they had to go on the top decks. This extra weight may have decreased her dubious stability.

She was commissioned by the Michigan Steamship Company and built by a local company specialising in cargo rather than passenger ships. The initial brief was to build a fast ship, capable of 20mph, carrying fruit and 500 passengers on the Great Lakes. This called for a long and lean vessel.

She got off to a bad start in her inaugural season in 1903: she struck a tugboat moored at the dock and sunk her. *Eastland* came off unharmed.

Worse still, the target speed promised was not met. Not only that, her draft was too deep for Michigan's shallow Black River. So, in her first year, back she went to the builder to make the modifications. This was the first of many made by a series of subsequent owners who put more emphasis on passenger numbers and less on carrying fruit and other cargo.

The Potato Mutiny

There is a difference between a strike and a mutiny, with the main one being that strikes are normally about workers' conditions whereas a mutiny is a bid to take over control. However, at sea any disinclination to follow orders could result in a charge of mutiny.

In 1906, on a voyage from Chicago to South Haven, six of the eight stokers on board *Eastland* were upset they were not served potatoes. After their requests were ignored, they downed shovels and refused to stoke the boilers. Captain John Pereue ordered the six of them to be arrested at gunpoint.

Eastland was able to continue on her way as the two other stokers kept the engine going until they reached South Haven. Here the stokers were charged with mutiny and taken to jail.

The result was that Captain Pereue was replaced and potatoes became available for stokers.

The progressive modifications made to *Eastland* had begun causing major listing problems. The builders claimed to have undertaken buoyancy and righting tests on launching that showed the ship would right after reaching an angle of 45°.

But many changes had been made to increase the number of passengers far beyond the original plan for 500. These included adding air conditioning and repositioning equipment to reduce the draft while increasing the weight. This was not a good combination.

Listing is caused by the ship being too top heavy, causing the centre of gravity to become too high. It is particularly noticeable during loading and unloading where, with weight being distributed, the ship reacts noticeably. We describe such ships as tender.

The successive owners were aware of the problem and some measures were taken to increase stability. After she nearly capsized in 1904, passenger numbers, which had grown to 3,000 rather than 500, were reduced to 2,800. Some passenger cabins were also removed. But the listing problem remained.

Eastland did have ballast tanks located low in the hull. These are used to flood with water to counter the listing effect. For instance, if the ship is listing to port, the starboard side tank is filled with water to act as a counterweight.

A List Too Far

Following the sinking of *Titanic* three years earlier, in 1915 the Federal Seamen's Act was passed and signed into law by President Woodrow Wilson. This set a minimum number of lifeboats that must be carried.

To meet these new requirements, *Eastland*'s owner, the St Joseph and Chicago Steamship Company, added lifeboats and rafts for 2,570 passengers. This made her even more top heavy.

The tendency is for passengers to gather on the upper decks to watch the embarkation, and as soon as the ship casts off, move to the other side of the ship to see what's happening. The combined weight of many passengers moving at the same time can have a large effect on the stability of a ship.

And so it was on 24 July 1915 when employees at Western Electric began to board for what was planned to be a workers' picnic.

The company had chartered four other steamers to take the entire staff for a day out in Michigan City. It was quite an event. However, before the ships got under way it quickly turned to tragedy.

It was an early start and a rainy morning. At 6.40 a.m., passengers began boarding, causing the ship to list to the starboard side. This was nearest the dock. *Eastland* pumped water into the opposite portside to even the ship out.

However, they must have overdone it because although the vessel straightened out, as soon as the passengers dispersed, the ship started to list even more to port. Again, adjustments were made to the ballast tanks and by 7.10 a.m. she had reached her passenger limit. The order was given to remove gangways and let go the mooring lines.

As she drifted clear of the docks, she was still listing to port. As passengers drifted over to the port side for a look, she took on a 25° list, causing water to flood the lower decks and dramatically alter the centre of gravity. At 7.28 a.m., and still only 7m from the dock, *Eastland* rolled over and came to rest on the bottom of the lake with the vessel half-submerged.

There were many passengers who, to escape the rain, had gone below. Suddenly, they found themselves under 20ft of water with pianos, book-cases and furniture falling on top of them. There was no way out.

On the upper decks, passengers and crew had more of a chance as a nearby vessel, *Kenosha*, quickly came alongside to allow them to leap to safety. Even though the police and fire departments were quickly on the scene, 844 passengers and four of the crew were killed in the accident. It was the deadliest day in Chicago's history.

The incident had the media baying for the blood of anyone in anyway connected to *Eastland*. This pressure caused the Western Electric Company to fork out $100,000 to be shared by family members of those taken by the disaster.

The investigations that followed prosecuted the owner and the crew. The case ended up in the Federal Court. It found that neither the crew, nor the owner of *Eastland* were liable since the ship had passed inspections and had been deemed seaworthy. The court also stated that *Eastland* 'was operated for years and carried thousands safely'. The people who certified the ship as seaworthy were not prosecuted. Nobody was to blame.

Born Again as USS *Wilmette*

This was not the end of *Eastland*; she was to rise again, and a new owner was sought. Two years later the US Navy, after anything that floated for the

First World War, converted her into a gunboat and entered her into service as USS *Wilmette*. However, that war ended before she saw action.

Her next duty was to serve as a training vessel on the Great Lakes for naval reservists. In June 1921 she was given the ceremonial task of sinking a German submarine surrendered to the United States after the First World War. The honour of sinking the U-boat was given to two gunner's mates, who, after the United States joined the conflict, fired the first cannon and the other fired the first American torpedo.

The US Navy was still using her during the Second World War. In August 1943, *Wilmette* carried President Franklin D. Roosevelt, Admiral William D. Leahy, James F. Byrnes and advisor Harry Hopkins on a ten-day cruise to plan war strategies.

After the war was over, the US had no further use for her and offered her for sale. There was no interest, and in 1946 she was sold for scrap.

10

SS *Andrea Doria*

SS *Andrea Doria*.

Born	1952
Died	1956
GRT	29,000
Length	700ft
Beam	90ft
Passengers	1,241
Crew	563
Line	Italian Line
Sister ship	SS *Cristoforo Colombo*

Tragedy in Fog

Stylish, modern and luxurious, this beautiful pride of Italy came to her sudden, dramatic end in one of the most horrendous and infamous marine disasters, after only five years of gracing the seas. Yet, thanks to the work of fine crews and rescuers, it eventuated in relatively little loss of life compared to the shocking reality of what might have happened.

During the Second World War, the Italian mercantile fleet was decimated. Italy, having changed sides a little after half-time, had her ships fall victim to both German and Allied attacks. What didn't sink, the Allies picked out as war reparations.

By the 1950s, the country was slowly shaking herself alive and the Italian spirit was again beginning to stand tall, proud and artistic. Previously a great maritime nation, Italy now began casting envious eyes over the prestigious grand liners from countries such as Britain, the Netherlands, Germany and France.

The Italians resolved to mark their re-entry with a grand flourish. Shunning the competition to be the biggest and grandest, they opted to go with a smaller ship, more adaptable to the emerging cruising market and with envy-making interiors, dripping with the very latest in stylish Italian décor. Think Ferrari, Dolce & Gabbana, Giorgio Armani, Versace, Prada and even Vespa. It's 1952, and entering stage right, dancing with delight, comes *Andrea Doria*, the first of near identical twins all set to be the finest ballerinas on the ocean waves.

Ships are not always given feminine names, but they are still mostly referred to as 'she', even when named after blokes. Andrea Doria was a Prince of Melfia, a swashbuckling sixteenth-century statesman, admiral and ruler of the Republic of Genoa. He lived a long, adventurous life and died at age 93. But, for the ship named after him, the allotted lifespan was to be much shorter.

The idea for the *Andrea Doria* and her sister ship, *Cristoforo Colombo*, which burst from her incubator three years later, was for them to run regular crossings on the balmier southern route across the Atlantic. This goes from New York to Gibraltar and then on through the Mediterranean, to stop at Cannes and Naples, before arriving back at Genoa. Opportunistic travel agents smartly labelled it the 'Sunny Southern Route'. It certainly sounds more attractive than a North Atlantic winter crossing.

Her interior was divided into three classes, with each section having its own swimming pool, dining room, lounges and enclosed promenade area. Along with a life-sized statue of Andrea Doria himself, more than $1 million was spent on artwork for the public rooms and cabins. That was when $1 million was worth a lot more than today. It sounds even better in lira: 1,736,660,000. And around that time, the size of each 1,000 lira note was just under 10in x 6in. A stack of those in your pocket and you really felt somebody.

But it was not all flash and glitz. Considerable attention was paid to safety with the formation of a double hull, eleven watertight compartments and enough lifeboats for all passengers and crew.

However, model testing had raised some listing issues when the ship was hit with force. This was quickly proved on her maiden voyage when a large wave smashed into her when off Nantucket and caused her to list 28°. This was significant. The watertight compartments only reached the top of A deck and a list of anything more than 20° would allow flood water to cascade over the top into adjacent compartments. Furthermore, such a list made the launching of lifeboats from the entire length of the raised side impossible. Half the lifeboats were gone in one hit.

Therefore, it was resolved at such times to ballast the empty fuel tanks with sea water as a safety precaution. However, this involves more complicated tank-cleaning procedures when in port and this is both costly and time-consuming.

Was this safety procedure forgotten or ignored when the *Andrea Doria* was nearing the end of her voyage in calm waters in July 1956?

Nantucket Fog

Just before midnight, *Andrea Doria* entered a thick Nantucket fog just hours from the safety of New York Harbor and crashed into an outgoing smaller cruise ship, *Stockholm*, at a steel-rendering combined collision speed of 40 knots, the equivalent of 46mph.

At a near 90° angle, the reinforced and sharply raked ice-breaking bow of the 12,000-ton Swedish American Line's *Stockholm* tore deep into *Andrea Doria*'s superstructure, ripping open five of the near-empty fuel tanks so they were exposed to the sea.

One passenger was thrown from her bed when her cabin was ripped open on *Andrea Doria* and she landed on *Stockholm*. She was found alive but injured.

On *Andrea Doria*, water immediately flooded below and began to pull her side down. Within minutes, likely exacerbated by the buoyancy of the five air-filled empty fuel tanks lifting her from the other side, the list exceeded 20°. With engines stopped, *Andrea Doria* engaged her pumps to level the ship by pumping water into the tanks on the high side, but the water intakes on the port side were now too high up for water to enter.

It was 11.10 p.m. and within thirty minutes it was realised the order would need to be given to abandon ship. Already the angle was so great that rather than embarking passengers on the promenade deck, the lifeboats would have to be lowered empty with passengers and crew left to scramble down to the water level on ropes and Jacob's ladders. Accordingly, the order was given for passengers to don their lifebelts, go to their lifeboat stations and await further instructions.

Both ships fell clear of each other with all engines stopped. The first 30ft of *Stockholm*'s bow was a crumpled maze of twisted steel. Her forward watertight compartment was flooded, and she was down at the bow. However, pumping out her forward water tanks brought her to near level. She was deemed to be in no imminent danger of sinking.

It was a different matter on *Andrea Doria*. There were 1,663 passengers and crew to be saved and it immediately became obvious that more lifeboats were urgently needed. A radio distress message was relayed to other ships calling all to assist.

First on scene was a freighter with limited lifeboats, then a US Navy transport ship followed by a US Navy destroyer, all with limited lifeboats but nevertheless able to use them to begin ferrying people in the water back to their ship.

Also hearing the distress call was the Europe-bound *Île de France*, the then pride of France on the US route. For her to turn back to the rescue would damage her proud, reliable transatlantic service record as she would need to refuel back in New York to complete her crossing. This would be a financial blow for French Line, but if her ship's lifeboats were needed then the captain felt duty-bound to help save lives.

Indeed, it was the *Ile de France*, shuttling her tenders back and forth between the two ships, who managed to rescue the bulk of the passengers.

Not only that, but some of her passengers were gracious enough to give up their cabins to the survivors.

Despite being badly damaged, *Stockholm* transported 545 survivors to New York under her own power. By 9.00 a.m., with the last of passengers and crew in lifeboats, *Andrea Doria*'s captain took his leave and an hour later the ship rolled and slipped bow first beneath the waves, just ten hours after the collision.

For an event of this magnitude, the death toll was surprisingly and thankfully low. The total was forty-six. On *Stockholm*, five were killed.

With all safely back ashore, the blame game began. Firstly, *Stockholm* shouldn't have been there. There are clearly defined and agreed shipping lanes and *Stockholm* was 20 miles north of the designated eastbound lane. This meant she was sailing directly into the path of westbound ships as well as entering an area notorious for its frequent thick banks of fog.

But it wasn't that the two ships hadn't seen each other, they had. Both spotted the other ship on their radar units but misinterpreted each other's courses. Neither had attempted radio contact to determine the other's exact heading.

When facing an oncoming collision situation, maritime regulations rule that both vessels should veer to starboard. In other words, keep right. But *Andrea Doria* was gradually steering to the left. When the situation became visually apparent, she attempted to outrun the collision by turning hard to port, while *Stockholm* tried to engage full astern while steering hard to starboard.

Brawling in open court would have done neither line any good. Complicating matters was the fact that Italian Line had to consider the reputation of its new sister ship, *Cristoforo Columbo*, while the Swedish *Stockholm* had her sister ship under construction in Italy. Both companies ended up distributing compensation funds for their own passengers and bearing their own legal costs.

Andrea Doria is now a very dangerous dive sight and as such has gone on to claim more deaths. The lure of diving on a sunken ship filled with many treasures has taken more than twenty lives.

11

TSMS *Lakonia*

(Formerly MS *Johan van Oldenbarnevelt*)

TSMS *Lakonia*.

Born	1930
Died	1963
GRT	19,040
Length	586ft
Beam	75ft
Passengers	770
Crew	376
Line	Greek Line

Unhappy Ending for Fun Ship

My first job on a passenger ship was junior photographer on board the ill-fated *Lakonia*. Cruising from Southampton, she used to take English passengers to the Mediterranean, Tangier and the Canary Islands.

With a slightly different spelling, *Lakonia* and her running mate, *Arkadia*, were often confused with Cunard ships having identical-sounding names. However, once on board, there was no doubting you were not on a Cunard ship.

I don't think Greek Line was trying to 'pass off' on Cunard because the names were Greek provinces. I guess they had as much right, if not more, to use those names.

Lakonia was the former Dutch ship *Johan van Oldenbarnevelt*, so maybe, even for the Greeks, the renaming was a much catchier alternative. She was a fun ship, continual wild parties for crew and passengers alike, and life on board was a real eye-opener for a naïve country boy like myself.

One favourite crew party venue was after hours in the hairdressing saloon. As soon as the last passenger's hairdo was completed, the bottles of lady's hair products were swept away to be replaced with bottles of booze and it became crew party central.

The photographers, shop staff, entertainment staff and hairdressers would keep the whole salon jumping into the early hours of the morning. It was a great shindig scene: disco lights flashing in the mirrors, rows of sinks crammed with ice and booze, a long row of seating for lolling about and, of course, the row of barber's chairs, which could hold three at a time.

I had never experienced such an intense party scene. It was a hotchpotch of people from all over the world, united by one common objective: to get into the booze and celebrate life. The passengers were there for fun, but the crew left them for dead. And it was full on every night.

The deck crews were also a very relaxed mob, who, during the day, would wander the boat deck wearing happy smiles and painting over any rust spots that appeared on the lifeboat's davits, chains and rigging. Lifeboat drills were often poorly attended and did not see the lifeboats raised or lowered into position. But they always looked very smart and shiny. I didn't know whether to be annoyed or relieved at the sight of one of them blocking most of the view from my boat deck cabin window.

But it was a great life on board, plus the fact she was popping in and out of my home port every eleven days. This was so much nicer than being stuck on ships far away for more than a year.

An Embarrassing Moment

Popping in and out of Southampton was convenient but we had to suffer continual customs inspections. When working on *Lakonia*'s sister ship, *Arcadia*, I had a birthday. In the carefree, casual approach to sex common on board ships, my mates were amused by my loyalty to my fiancée back home and found my shy on-board celibacy a source of great amusement. Accordingly, for a giggle, they presented me with a big carton containing a gross of what we used to call French letters. All right, in these less euphemistic times: condoms.

I don't know if you've ever seen a gross of French letters, but I can assure you it is not something to slip into your wallet or pop into the back pocket. It is big, bulky and, quite frankly, embarrassing. In fact, just as my dear friends had intended.

I dutifully took the box back to my cabin and, knowing I was having VIP shore visitors the next day, stowed it behind a pile of dirty washing at the bottom of my wardrobe.

In the morning we docked, and straight aboard came my boss from London, my parents and my young and innocent intended. They crowded into my tiny cabin, albeit with a little bit of jiggling and shuffling. When everyone was settled, I shyly went ahead with my report to my boss in front of my loved ones, putting all my papers on my small table and going through the business details of the trip just completed.

There came a knock on the door and squeezing into the tiny space left in my cabin came the two biggest British customs officers I have ever seen. Both were carrying large torches and long sticks with mirrors on the end. They decided to do a full search of my cabin.

Manfully, I carried on with my voyage report, but all eyes were watching the two customs officers as they pulled out the drawers beneath my bunk and started poking torches and mirrors into every conceivable hiding place. As I struggled on in this uncomfortable atmosphere, my boss, mum, dad and fiancée had all eyes swivelled to the customs officers, watching their every move.

Inevitably they came to the cupboard where I had hidden the box of French letters. As they went through my hanging clothes, memory of what I had hidden came flooding back. As I watched them starting to pick through my pile of dirty washing, my cheeks burned red. Up came the carton and as it was still sealed, the leader turned to me and asked what was in it.

I was now flushing madly and said the stupidest thing one could ever say to a customs officer.

'I wouldn't look in there if I were you,' stammered this idiot.

He gave me a pitying look, ripped open the box and dramatically poured out its contents onto the coffee table. Down they came, shining and glinting in their individual foil wrapping, all over my business papers and spilling over onto the floor.

There was a moment of dead silence. There was a definite frisson in the air while everyone considered the possible implications of what they saw. Now all eyes were on me.

'It was a gift,' I stumbled. Nobody believed me. They were wondering just what sort of person needs to carry 144 condoms.

Despite this, I enjoyed the Greek ships and I was truly disappointed when I was transferred from *Lakonia* to another ship just before the much-anticipated Christmas cruise.

Missing the Disaster

In 1963 she sailed from Southampton with 1,027 passengers and crew on board. It was without me. And it was the last voyage she was ever to make.

My position was taken by another new photographer. Like me, he had started his career taking mainly press photos, so when three days into the cruise fire broke out, he sprang into action. Grabbing his camera, he raced around the boat deck photographing the conflagration taking hold and the passengers hurling themselves over the rails to escape the flames. He was everywhere and on the scoop of the century.

The fire had started in that hairdressing salon and, with all the chemicals about, it spread rapidly out of control. When the time came to head for the lifeboats, it was discovered many had the gear wheels painted over so thickly the boats could not be lowered.

My replacement photographer perished in the fire along with 127 others. About half were killed by fire, the others by drowning or by jumping into the water from the boat deck and breaking their necks.

As I had been a former contributor, I found fame in my local newspaper for having missed the disaster. Always the local angle. They ran a headline to say I had missed the disaster, and thereafter, any mention of me was prefixed with the words, 'Paul Curtis, who narrowly missed the *Lakonia* disaster ...'

My most treasured clipping was the news of my marriage to a New Zealand lass. This was reported as, 'Paul Curtis, who narrowly missed the *Lakonia* disaster, was married on Saturday ...' They might have been percipient, as fifty years later that marriage also went up in flames.

However, the *Lakonia* disaster was not the end of the Greek Line. A year or so later, I was transferred to *Arkadia*. Following the same cruise route as *Lakonia*, the captain would always call me to the bridge to photograph a ceremony where he would stop his ship at the spot *Lakonia* sunk, say a prayer and then drop a wreath into the sea. On his ship, for the whole cruise, lifeboats kept going up and down like yo-yos.

Such is the relationship between some crew members and their ship, not all automatically leave when she sails under new owners. This is particularly true of the engineers. In the instance of *Lakonia*, a former and original engineer under Dutch ownership was still looking after his beloved engines. And the number of foreign-flagged vessels with a Scotsman hidden away in the engine room is amazing.

Working for the Dutch

Johan van Oldenbarnevelt was built for the Netherland Steamship Company, or Holland America Line as we now know it. She was named after a famous sixteenth-century soldier who fought bravely for Dutch independence and then made the mistake of getting into politics.

As has often been quoted, 'war's a dirty business but politics ... my god!' Add in religion and you have truly found hell. For his patriotic endeavours, he was tried by a kangaroo court and beheaded at The Hague by his countrymen at the age of 71.

The ship, whose name, to the relief of all, was popularly shortened to *JVO*, began operating services, both passenger and cargo, between

Amsterdam and the Dutch East Indies, now known as Indonesia. When the Second World War began, she switched to being a cargo ship running between Batavia (think Jakarta) and New York City. In 1941, she was converted to be a troopship servicing India, Singapore and Penang.

She survived the war and resumed her Amsterdam to Batavia route, fairing much better than her sister ship, *Marnix van St Aldegonde*, which was torpedoed and sunk by German aircraft.

When Indonesia became independent, *JVO* abandoned the East Indies service to travel a bit further and carried migrants to Australia and New Zealand. Later, she began a series of world cruises.

After thirty-three successful years with the Dutch, she was sold to operate for Greek Line in March 1963 to run cruises from Southampton to the Canary Islands. It was only a few months later that the fatal fire broke out.

As it spread it was decided to sound the fire alarms, but they could only be heard faintly, in all probability because they had been painted over. Only half the lifeboats could be launched, and they were heavily overcrowded.

After all who could had abandoned the ship, ocean tugs took *Lakonia* under tow to Gibraltar. However, she never made it as, five days later and while still in the Atlantic, she developed a list and sank 230 miles south-west of Lisbon.

The board of inquiry report found fault with the maintenance of equipment, thoroughness of lifeboat drills and the standard of supervision. It was also determined that the order to abandon ship had been given too late and many of the officers and crew were guilty of not properly handling the evacuation. This resulted in eight of the ship's officers being charged with negligence.

12

RMS *Mauretania*

RMS *Mauretania*.

Born	1939
Died	1965
GRT	35,738
Length	772ft
Beam	89ft
Passengers	1,360
Crew	802
Line	Cunard Line

'Getting There is Half the Fun'

The first Cunard ship I ever boarded was *Mauretania*. I was standing on the dock, camera in hand, admiring the classical beauty of her lines and how smart she looked with her dark hull, white topsides and famous black-banded red funnels. She was a slightly smaller version of *Queen Elizabeth*, and truth be told, she looked the better for it.

Two attractive ladies came along and stopped to watch me taking pictures. 'That,' they said, 'is the best ship in the world.'

'No,' I replied, pointing a bit further down New York's famous Liner Row to my own ship, 'That is.'

We struck up a lively and teasing conversation about the relative merits of our two ships.

It turned out they had been working in the ship's gift shops for years and it was clear how much in love they were with what they referred to as the 'Old Maurie'. They were ten years older than me and they expressed fears that both the ship's and thus their own cruising days would soon end.

'Come on,' they said. 'You'd better have a look while you can.' And took me aboard.

Two beautiful ladies and a wonderful ship. How could I say no. In the early 1960s, popping on and off other crew members' ship was a very simple affair. Often security went to the extent of leaving a master of arms at the top of the gangway, but if you approached in a hurry and looked like you knew where you were going, you were rarely challenged.

If dressed in the uniform of another ship, or you carried your seaman's card, you were generally warmly welcomed. It was the courtesy of the sea. Marching up the gangway between the arms of two glamorous and well-known crew members presented no problems, except for maybe an envious glance.

Exuding energy and excitement, they took me all around the ship's late art deco lounges and the wide-open decks, before ending up in a bar to exchange tales of sea life over numerous rum and cokes.

When I staggered back down the gangway, I was in love. Both with the two women and their wonderful ship. She was a classic example of how a ship can inspire a crew with pride, love and enthusiasm.

Her predecessor, the first *Mauretania*, who died in 1935, was also much loved and had gathered an enormous amount of crew and passenger goodwill.

The shipping company wanted to capitalise on this, so when the first *Mauretania* retired, to keep the name in the Registry of Ships, Cunard persuaded Red Funnel Steamers to rename one of its boats as *Mauretania* until the new one could be built.

The new *Mauretania* was the first ship to be built out of the union of Cunard and White Star Line and was ordered from Cammell Laird at Birkenhead, making her the largest liner at that time to be built at an English shipyard. Previous liners had mostly been built in Scotland or Ireland.

She was built for the Southampton to New York run, but just four months after she commenced her scheduled crossings, the news came that Germany had invaded Poland.

Getting There With a Gun

Mauretania was ordered to travel straight to Southampton, and not make her usual call at Cobh. She arrived on the very day war was declared.

She was immediately requisitioned by the British Government, armed with weapons, including two 6in guns, painted in battleship grey and sent back to the neutral United States. She sat in New York's Liner Row for three months, alongside *Queen Elizabeth*, *Queen Mary* and *Normandie*.

Mauretania's later advertising pitch, 'Getting there is half the fun', was a slogan quickly entered into common usage. It was a dig at her direct competitor: airline travel. Later, business author Robert C. Townsend took the slogan one step further, saying, 'Getting there isn't half the fun, it's all the fun.'

However, I doubt her new wartime passengers would have been overly enamoured with either slogan. For conversion to a troopship she was sent via Panama to Sydney, Australia.

After conversion, she left Sydney with 2,000 troops on board, as part of one of the largest convoys ever assembled. Convoy US3 included the troop transports *Queen Mary*, *Aquitania*, *Empress of Britain*, *Empress of Japan* and *Andes*. Mostly, Her Majesty's Ship (HMT) *Aquitania*, as she was now called, served in the North Atlantic, but she also served in the Pacific.

On her very last voyage as a troopship she brought home Field Marshall Viscount Montgomery. After that she became the first war bride ship, reuniting English war brides and their children with the Canadian troops they had married while they were stationed in England. Ironically, on the way back to Liverpool, *Mauretania* carried 2,752 prisoners of war.

Finally, in September 1946, the British Government handed her back to Cunard. The company immediately restored her to her pre-war condition and sent her off on only her second run to New York in peace time.

A couple of years later, *Mauretania* abandoned the winter months of Atlantic crossing in favour of cruising. For this, she abandoned the class system and only carried 750 passengers.

Her cruising brought in lots of US dollars, which were much needed for Britain's war-shattered economy. In 1957, she was given another refit and received partial air conditioning for the Caribbean cruises.

With the airlines dominating the Atlantic crossing trade, the company decided to switch her more and more to cruising. In 1962, Cunard gave her a complete makeover, air-conditioned the whole ship and spruced up her interior fittings. As they wanted to signal she was now a cruise ship, they painted her that appalling sickly green colour used on *Caronia* and the Liverpool trams. She certainly lost a lot of her style. I think I would have preferred her to stay in battleship grey.

She cruised the Caribbean and the Mediterranean but increasing operating costs and the age of the ship made Cunard include her in a major 1960s sale of a large part of the fleet. Deemed too old for further life as a cruise ship, she suffered the indignity of having to be sold for scrap. In 1965, with Captain Treasure Jones in command, *Mauretania* was nosed into the breaker's yard in Scotland.

Captain Treasure Jones pulled the engine room telegraph to 'Finished with Engines'. He was to become good at this. In Los Angeles, just two years later, he did the same thing on *Queen Mary*, but instead of for scrapping it was for the highly preferable role of being made into a hotel ship.

13

SS *Queen of Bermuda*

SS *Queen of Bermuda*. (Courtesy of © Stephen J. Card, from an original colour painting)

Born	1933
Died	1966
GRT	22,575
Length	169ft
Beam	77ft
Passengers	733
Line	Furness Bermuda Line

Honeymooners' Delight

Invariably, on many a cruise ship you just have time to catch breakfast, then you're off ashore, running around some wonderful exotic port, then dashing back in time for dinner or the ship will sail without you. The next morning you repeat the same exercise in a different place. Alas, this means you miss out on all the fun of seeing the town in the evening, when offices disgorge their workers and the place comes alive with something other than just tourists. If you've already left, there's no opportunity to drink with the locals, eat in their restaurants or hit the night life.

There are two main reasons for this, both financial. The cruise companies find it cheaper to give you dinner and have you spending in their bars and gambling in their casinos. The company also saves on port dues.

There is another practical reason. Back in the 1960s, when we often made late-night departures, some of the crew would invariably end up being seduced by alcohol and other delights and not get back to the ship in time. It might take a day or two for the missing crew to get repatriated. As it could inconvenience some passenger services, this was punished severely. The miscreants might try to sneak aboard in the next port, but invariably they were caught. I know!

This is not to say that these days all ships, all the time, always leave port around 6 p.m. There are exceptions to this rule, but generally such cruises tend to cost a bit more.

The idea of the ship being your hotel in port was never better executed than by Furness Bermuda Line with its *Queen of Bermuda* and *Ocean Monarch*. For decades they used to run six-day summer cruises from New York City, spend one full day at sea, and then tie up right on the main street of Bermuda's Hamilton and stay there for three whole days. And no sooner had one of the sisters left to go back to New York, the other arrived. Practically, this meant the prized docking in the main street was always occupied by one of their two ships and the rest of us, on other arriving ships, used to end up anchored or docked in less-attractive spots.

Cash for Cashmere

I always wanted to spend a few months working that run. For a ship's photographer, there would be not much to do when the ship was in Hamilton and all the passengers were ashore. So, there would be loads of time off and where better to spend it than on that wonderful island of Bermuda. It is more British than Britain.

As it was, I did often make one-day stopovers on our way to the Caribbean. The island in those days had strict censorship laws and there was a healthy demand for copies of D.H. Lawrence's newly released *Lady Chatterley's Lover*. Back in New York I would buy six copies and smuggle the banned books ashore in Bermuda. I don't think I was ever paid in cash, but, delivering them to a pub, I would spend long, convivial hours drinking good English beer and tucking into fine roast beef and Yorkshire pudding without ever being asked for a penny.

The six-day cruises certainly also turned a tidy profit for Furness Withy and Bermuda itself. The locals used to call it the millionaires' cruises as it brought many big-spending Americans delighted to find a little bit of Oxford Street comparatively close to their doorstep. Cashmere, Royal Doulton and Wedgwood were all the rage in the shops, and passengers took them away by the suitcase load.

The Furness ships were also ideal for honeymooners. With little time at sea and much time stationary in port, there was little fear of sea sickness ruining the celebrations.

The run was not pioneered by *Queen of Bermuda*. She was ordered by Furness Withy to replace its MV *Bermuda*, which, after only a little more than three years' service, burst into flames. So the three-funnelled *Queen* began her run in tandem with *Monarch of Bermuda* in 1933.

Both millionaires and honeymooners were forced to look for alternative venues for their amusement when the British Admiralty requisitioned both ships for Second World War duty. SS *Queen of Bermuda* was renamed on 28 October (my birthday, please take note) as His Majesty's Ship (HMS) *Queen of Bermuda*.

Along with the new prefix, the Admiralty made her into an armed merchant cruiser and gave her seven naval guns and two anti-aircraft guns. The aft funnel was removed to give a clearer field of fire. It also made sure they didn't shoot it off themselves. It was only a dummy, but it did contain the radio room.

Dummy funnels were not unusual at the time as it was thought the more funnels, the more prestige. On one ship, the third funnel was used as a solarium for nude sunbathing.

Queen of Bermuda was refitted as a troopship in 1943 and carried soldiers from Britain to Mediterranean ports. With the war over, she took Italian prisoners of war in Britain back to Naples. Her last duty was to bring home British troops from the Far East.

In 1947 the UK Government relinquished her back to Furness Withy, which refitted her and put back the third funnel. In February 1949, she was given a warm welcome back on her pre-war route between New York and Hamilton.

Not so lucky was her former running mate, *Monarch of Bermuda*. She was damaged by fire in a shipyard during her renovations from war service. The company decided to sell her and after some major work she sailed again: first as *New Australia*, and then later as the Greek Line's *Arkadia*. In this, her last role, I worked on her for a while as the manager of the photo unit and a gift shop. I had the time of my life, but that's another story.

Queen of Bermuda's new running mate, *Ocean Monarch* arrived in 1951, slightly smaller but still a very good ship. The good days continued for these glamour ships. They carried passengers such as Doris Day, Noël Coward and Howard Truman. They also carried English pop star Tommy Steele, but he was working as a bellboy and taking part in the crew shows.

Famous marine artist Stephen J. Card and co-author Piers Plowman say that afternoon tea required 7,500 cups, saucers and teapots. Sometimes, the crew, in their hurry to get ashore, would throw some of the china overboard into Hamilton Island harbour. Later, divers happened upon them and collected them from the seabed, explaining why Royal Doulton crockery is found in many Bermudian homes.

Trying to keep their long run in good order, in 1961 they sent *Queen of Bermuda* off to Harland & Wolff in Belfast for a complete makeover. First, they lengthened her, and then they took away two of her three funnels. This possibly made her the only passenger liner in the world to sail at different times with one, two and three funnels. She was a ship spotter's worst nightmare.

Rising fuel prices, maintenance costs and battles with the airlines, eventually took their toll on *Queen of Bermuda*. This glorious ship was reluctantly sold for scrap in 1966.

14

RMS *Queen Elizabeth*

RMS *Queen Elizabeth*. (Author)

Born	1938
Died	1972
GRT	83,673
Length	1,031ft
Beam	118ft
Passengers	2,283
Crew	1,000
Line	Cunard Line
Sister ship	*Queen Mary*

Queen of the Atlantic

Born on the heels of the success of *Queen Mary*, the design process for the new ship, *Queen Elizabeth*, was easier and benefited from seeing the *Mary* in practice. For further ideas, Cunard sent a spy posing as a passenger on board *Normandie*. He said he was a grocer, but, with some of the detailed, technical questions he was asking, he must have raised a few French eyebrows. Why would a seller of sacks of potatoes want to know the inside measurement of the aft smokestack?

With an eye to votes, the British Government, basking in the glory of *Queen Mary*'s success and not wanting to see unemployment return to the Clyde, was forthcoming with financial help for the building of the new ship. The building contract was again signed with John Brown's shipyard and at the end of 1936 work began. While there were 3,000 welding and riveting at the shipyard, the need for components, furnishings and fittings spread many other employment opportunities across Britain. Altogether, a quarter of a million people were employed on the project.

The queen herself did the christening honours on 27 September 1938. The king had to cry off, as he felt he couldn't leave London at a time when Britain was on the brink of war with Germany.

Queen Elizabeth was more than up to the job as when the vital moment came, and the tide was at its peak, the ship started to slide on its own down the slipway. The queen quickly pressed the release button to the champagne bottle, just in time for it to break against the last part of the bow.

Elizabeth looked quite different from *Mary*. She was 12ft longer and with only two funnels, she had one fewer than her sister. This was made possible by improved engineering and allowed the giant ventilators on *Mary*'s top deck to be eliminated to give more room on the new ship's sports deck.

Elizabeth, quickly and affectionately renamed by the crew as the *Lizzie*, also had finer bows with a more pronounced rake, while the foredeck was fitted flush with the bow. A massive V-shaped, steel breakwater on this deck protected the ship from being swept by any huge, head-on seas.

She had the same beam as *Mary*, but her gross tonnage made her 2,436 tons larger. Those of us working on *Mary* considered this a very minor play at one-upmanship and we were a better, friendlier ship with a smarter crew. And hell, we had the extra funnel.

For her maiden sailing from England there was no hoopla. Britain was now at war, so it was done in secret. No cheering crowds, no media and no fire tugs spewing huge plumes of water high into the air. Instead, *Elizabeth* slunk out of her Clydeside fitting-out basin under 20 tons of camouflage grey paint and a dark cloak of secrecy.

With only a skeleton crew on board, everyone thought she was bound for the Southampton dry dock to load the furnishings and other supplies already sent there. But this was just a cunning ploy and subterfuge by the Brits to fool the Germans.

And it did. Waves of Luftwaffe aircraft were seen flying all over the Southampton approaches, but there was no big new ship to bomb. For instead of sailing south as everyone surmised, *Elizabeth* was sailing west, flat out for the neutral port of New York.

This didn't only take the Germans by surprise; it also gave the crew the shock of their lives. It was only on the day of sailing that the captain opened sealed orders from Winston Churchill directing him to head at full speed directly for New York.

With no idea this possibility was in the offing, at the last minute the workmen and crew were given a chance to leave. But British spirit came to the fore. With not even a toothbrush or a change of clothing, most opted to stay and thus suddenly found themselves off to the States. So, they were a bit late home for dinner that night. For many, it was more than a year before they could get back to Britain.

From Luxury Liners to Troopships

To Cunard's distress, by the time *Elizabeth* was a day out of New York, the news of her escape had leaked out. As she was docking, massive crowds swarmed the piers to see her for the first time. This was not good news for Cunard as sabotage agents were everywhere. They were to be blamed for the fiery death of the great French Liner *Normandie* while she was meant to be nice and secure in her berth in New York.

All the rumours say it was deliberate arson. Even so, I say it was pure stupidity. As with the *Normandie* and other ships, she met the same fate of having fire boats arrive and pour tons of water until she filled up and inevitably rolled over. A total write-off.

With the war finished, a crowded ship brings American troops
back to New York in 1945.

New York now had the world's two largest liners in its port and tensions were running high. What to do with them?

The first step was to fit both Queens with anti-magnetic coils to protect against mines. The idea here was to explode the mines before they got close enough to damage the ship. Erm.

They also had a mine-sweeping system that consisted of streaming a torpedo-shaped device on strong cables either side of the ship. The theory was the cables would cut the anchor lines attaching the mines to the sea bottom and cause them to float to the surface. There, says the manual, they could be safely exploded by a rear-mounted gunner. The game of Russian roulette comes to mind.

For the conversion work to troopships, the two Queens were first sent to Cape Town and then for further work onto Sydney, Australia. By the spring of 1941, the conversion work was finished and a total of 11,600 Australian soldiers were taken aboard the two ships for transfer to the battle fronts. Thus her trooping days began.

During the war, it was humour, albeit often grim, that kept everyone going. Once, in the Red Sea, *Queen Elizabeth* passed the battleship of the British Navy called HMS *Queen Elizabeth*. Up went the signal flags with a laconic one word greeting: 'Snap'.

Churchill said the role played by the Queens shortened the war by two years.

On the Peacetime Run

With the war over, *Queen Elizabeth* was able to begin her scheduled crossing service with *Queen Mary*. It was a dynamic partnership. Both Queens were carrying celebrities, rich businessmen and tourists. The officers and crew had to swiftly amend their approach to the new passengers. These were not conscripts on their way to war, but service-demanding, rich and successful passengers able to choose between a number of competing shipping companies.

Interviewed at the time by the *New Yorker* magazine, Commodore James Bisset was asked if it was not something of a let-down to command *Elizabeth* on a peacetime run. With his dry humour, Bisset answered, 'Oh aye. But not so bad. We've no bombs and torpedoes, but we do have the passengers.'

In the 1960s, some passengers would elegantly stroll the decks, but most seemed content to sit on the promenade deck in their steamer chairs, wrapped in warmed blankets and drinking their hot bouillon. At other times you could find them sitting in the lounges, or in the pursers' lobby, indulging in the favourite sport of people watching.

As an entertainment officer, part of my job was to 'bumble' the passengers. This was Cunard speak for spotting lonely looking passengers and going over for a little chat, or perhaps to buy them a drink on the company. So, a great deal of my day was spent mumbling and bumbling along.

There were meetings to host for various interest groups such as Kiwanis, Masons, Rotarians and Lions. Of course, there was also the daily game of bridge, but in those days, an eye had to be kept out for professional gamblers who criss-crossed the Atlantic plying their card-sharping tricks for a living.

On the modern Queens, strictly controlled casinos provide all forms of gambling. Even the betting on the daily mileage run has been abandoned.

Gone is the nautical chart displayed so passengers could wager on the next day's noon position. This practice was abandoned after passengers started arriving armed with portable GPS units and smartphones.

Our standard evening entertainment was the dance band, with the main excitement coming from novelty dancing, such as passing the broomstick or musical chairs. Exciting stuff.

On one night, we would have the traditional fancy-dress competition with its regular parade of Charlie Chaplins, Carmen Mirandas and King Neptunes. We saw the same character impersonations each trip, probably because passengers mostly used the limited range of dress-up materials we offered.

On another night, we held our own brand of horseracing. This consisted of six painted wooden horse and jockey silhouettes mounted on small stands. Two smart sailors would move the horses along a track made of green velvet and marked out with furlong lines.

Every evening we would call bingo. In those days, this was done by having a small bag containing numbered plastic discs. A lady passenger would be invited on stage to shake the bag so that the emcee could reach in and pull out a number to call bingo style: 'Quack-quack, two little ducks in the water; two and two, twenty-two; whichever way you look at it, sixty-nine.' Painful wasn't it!

If their numbers were not coming out, players would frequently yell out 'shake the bag'. So, bingo was quite a raucous affair; unlike today, where it is mostly played in stony silence.

While we had occasional performances by the big names working their way across the Atlantic, mostly the entertainment and its presentation was very basic. It was nothing like today's Queens with their West End-style theatres and teams of technicians sitting in glassed-in bio booths controlling raising stages, moving curtains, elaborate lighting and extensive sound systems.

The dance band was on a low stage at the back of the dance floor. A couple of scrubbed up and smartly dressed deckhands would each man a single follow spotlight shining each side of a detachable stand microphone shared by both compere and performer.

As for the ship's disco, there were no smooth-pattered DJs operating fog machines, booming speakers, rows of turntables, mixing desks and flickering lights. Just a big monster jukebox and an entertainment officer with a bag full of sixpences to drive it.

It was great fun to be on the Queens. We had to work hard, but in those days we generally had three, four and sometimes five turnaround days in

New York and Southampton. There was none of that same-day turnaround nonsense ships must endure these days. We really had time to relax and explore at the end of every five-day trip.

The advent of jet travel was to end it all. First *Queen Mary* went in 1967 and *Queen Elizabeth* was only to last another twelve months on the North Atlantic before being sold off to Philadelphia buyers for $7.5 million.

In a joint venture she was transferred to act as a hotel and tourist attraction in Port Everglades. She lost her crown and became simply called *Elizabeth*. She did not fare well in the hot climate and, besides, from the novelty perspective, one thing that Florida port is not short of is a big passenger ship to look at.

She was towed to Hong Kong when Tung Chao Young bought her for US$3.5 million. He insured her for $8 million as he was going to spend $5 million converting her to a seagoing university. In a play on the new owner's initials, C.Y., she was renamed *Seawise University*.

However, the conversion work was making slow progress when, in June 1972, the ship caught fire in several places at once. Fire boats came to the rescue, but, as with the end of *Normandie* in New York, they made the same mistake of pouring gallons and gallons of water over her until she capsized and sank. Some suspected arson or sabotage.

For some years, with her blackened superstructure still visible above the water in Hong Kong Harbour, she was a heartbreaking sight. Two years later, and with no rescue possible, the top parts of the ship were broken up for scrap and the remains on the seabed marked on nautical charts as a hazard to navigation.

Ironically, two of the ship's brass plates showing, of all things, the fire warning system, were recovered and are now on display in the Hong Kong Aberdeen Boat Club. The Parker Pen Company seized the opportunity of using the salvage material from *Elizabeth* to make a limited edition of 5,000 pens.

Something similar happened to *Queen Mary*, but it was just a case of melting down a spare propeller stored near Southampton. It was made of manganese, brass and bronze, was 20ft in diameter and weighed 35 tons. An enterprising scrap merchant bought it for very little money and turned it into thousands of souvenir drink coasters that sold for very much. I know, I have some.

However, it was just a propeller, and an unused one at that. While the fate of *Queen Mary* is not necessarily ideal, it certainly beats ending up as a few Parker pens.

15

RMS *Caronia*
(Later SS *Columbia* and SS *Caribia*)

RMS *Caronia*. (Oskar A. Johansen, via Flickr CC A 2.0)

Born	1948
Died	1974
GRT	34,274
Length	715ft
Beam	91ft
Passengers	932
Crew	695
Line	Cunard Line

The Green Goddess of Cruising

In my teens, my seagoing ambition was for a job on *Caronia*. At the time, it was the biggest and best cruise ship and voyaged the entire world. The appeal was slightly dimmed by the decision to paint her in an appalling sick-inducing four shades of green.

Cunard was originally based in Liverpool and wanted the new ship to be different from their traditional black-hulled transatlantic liners. They succeeded. In choosing green, they came under the influence of the city's proudly green trams. In Liverpool, that paint must have been going cheap. However, most, it seems, were happy with the new colour scheme and we admit it made her cooler in tropical waters. She was nicknamed the Green Goddess, but then, so were the trams.

Granted, Liverpool's trams looked good on the city's grey streets, but to call a magnificent liner after a tram doesn't seem quite right to ship lovers. Besides, *Caronia*'s funnel alone was so wide it could house three of those trams side by side.

When *Queen Mary* was coming to the end of her career, and thus mine as her cabin-class entertainment officer, Cunard first offered to transfer me to the 19-year-old *Caronia*. At last! But before I could pack my bag, both the ship and my offer were withdrawn. That's life.

A Forward-Thinking Baronet

The idea for such a luxury cruise ship came from Sir Percy Bates. He took the helm as chairman of Cunard in 1930 and in the boardroom faced his own storms. First the Great Depression with its roaring inflationary costs, and then the government forced a merger with Cunard's bitter rival, the White Star Line. Only then would the government assist in the difficult building of *Queen Mary* and *Queen Elizabeth*.

Sir Percy was one of the first to say transatlantic liners would one day face a challenge from air travel. Indeed, at one stage Cunard prepared to enter the airline business, but the government did not want them competing with what we now know as British Airways.

He ordered *Caronia* to be built as a ship capable of making year-round transatlantic crossings, but also equally at home cruising the world. In other words, it was a two-way bet.

This commission was met with a smaller ship of less draft and more speed than the two Queens. She was claimed to be the first big purpose-built cruise ship in the world. The single funnel was the widest at sea and housed six very large draught fans for the boilers. It helped keep the decks free and certainly gave her a very distinctive look.

Caronia claimed several firsts. She was the first with private bathrooms for each cabin. The crew were not quite so lucky. She was also the first to have a permanent outdoor pool, terraced aft decks and large picture windows. For transatlantic runs she could be separated into first and cabin class, but for cruising, which she came to do most of the time, she was entirely first class.

She was Cunard's second ship to be named *Caronia* and was launched in October 1947 by Princess Elizabeth. This was her last public engagement before she married Prince Philip and became queen.

The ship's maiden voyage in 1949 was a run to New York. She made three of these before beginning a series of cruises from New York to the Caribbean. She began her first world cruise in 1951.

Finding success in the cruise market, she was air-conditioned throughout and switched to full-time cruising for ten months of the year. Offering impeccable service, Cunard would fly in fresh supplies, such as fresh milk or lobsters, for her arrival in foreign ports.

It led to a life a few found hard to resist, with an occasional passenger taking up permanent residence on board. For instance, there was Clara Macbeth, a lady who lived on board for fifteen years, notching up a total travel bill of $20 million.

Passengers used to vie with each other to put on the best and most lavish private party. Small wonder the Green Goddess became referred to as the millionaire's yacht.

Front-Row Seats for the Coronation

The Brits are very good at putting on a 'bit of a do' and when it came to the coronation of Queen Elizabeth, they pulled out all the stops. For the ceremony, they crammed into Westminster Abbey 8,251 guests representing 129 nations and territories.

Just under 30,000 men from the armed forces took part in the procession and 8,000 various types of police were brought in to supplement London's regular Metropolitan force. After all, they had to handle 3 million spectators crammed along the coronation route. Some of the public had camped overnight to secure a good spot. Into this melee throw 200 journalists and 500 photographers reporting in thirty-nine languages to ninety-two nations. Apple store openings: eat your heart out.

Every hotel in Britain was booked out, so how to bring in 500 Americans wanting to join the fun? Enter *Caronia* on a special Coronation Cruise, diverting from the Mediterranean to serve as a hotel ship in Southampton to let passengers catch the train to London for the big day.

Of course, *Caronia* passengers were not expected to join the hoi polloi crowding the streets and straining for a view on that rainy day. They were provided with reserved seats in a specially built, roofed viewing stand in a premier position at London's Hyde Park Corner.

However, seeing the coronation required an early start. London's streets began closing off hours before the Royal Procession was to begin. Accordingly, at 4 a.m. and 4.15 a.m., *Caronia* passengers boarded two Pullman trains for the journey to London.

It was a long day with the party not getting back to the ship until after 9 p.m. But the passengers experienced the event of their lives. To commemorate the coronation, like every other schoolchild in Britain, all I got was a ruddy mug.

Trouble in Yokohama

How many electricians does it take to change a light bulb? Well in the case of *Caronia*'s aft navigation light mounted on top of the funnel, it took just one. But it was the worst job on the ship. The electrician would take a service lift to the top deck, open a secret door in the base of the funnel and, once inside, climb a ladder to the top. Because of the foul air going out the funnel, he had to hold his breath for as long as possible and get out as soon as he could. Today's health and safety inspectors would never pass that.

The huge, wide funnel also created difficulty manoeuvring in port. When moving slowly, its windage easily swayed *Caronia* off course. It took great skill to dock her perfectly.

One day in 1958, she was leaving Yokohama in her usual style: bands playing, streamers flying, fireworks exploding and big crowds cheering.

It's all very well being sent off in such grand manner, but if something goes wrong, imagine how it must feel to those on the bridge.

This day, the wind was blowing strongly as two tugs at the bow and three astern pulled her clear of the dock. No sooner was she in the channel, than the tugs astern retrieved their lines and took off. This caused consternation on the bridge. It is usual for tugs to travel in attendance until a ship is clear of the port. But they were still just under a mile short of the narrow breakwater entrance.

As *Caronia* neared the breakwater, a very large US Navy tank landing craft carrier began to enter from the opposite direction. Again, this is not standard practice. A vessel entering a narrow harbour should give way to one leaving. However, it seems those on the 5,000-ton tank carrier were unaware of this. They were more intent on getting a close look at *Caronia* and blissfully unaware they were pushing the ship down onto a lee shore.

On the bridge a quick decision had to be made. Either carry on and hit the tank landing craft and risk it tearing a long hole in the side of the ship and possibly sinking *Caronia* or slow the ship and risk the wind getting hold of the funnel and sailing her into the breakwater. They chose the risk of hitting the breakwater.

She hit with a hard jolt and a big bang, crumpling the bow. Passenger alarms were sounded, and they scurried for their life jackets. On the breakwater, three people in the harbour light tower saw the giant ship coming at them, jumped out and began running for their lives.

As she was pulled clear, her anchor hit the light tower and sent it crashing to the ground. But the integrity of *Caronia*'s hull remained sound.

She immediately returned for repairs at the US Navy dockyard. Even though it was not *Caronia*'s fault, Cunard also had to fork out for the repairs to the breakwater and light tower.

The Sorry Rebirth as *Caribia*

By 1965, other shipping companies were building their own purpose-built cruise ships and the time had come for *Caronia* to play catch-up. They put her into dry dock for a three-month overhaul, adding new accommodation suites, a new lido deck and a complete interior makeover.

However, it was too little too late. By 1967, the British seamen's strike, coupled with the airlines dominating the travel business, had Cunard haemorrhaging money. The decision was made to sell *Queen Mary*, *Queen Elizabeth*, *Caronia*, *Carinthia* and *Sylvania*.

Tied up in a long line, the ships were docked side by side at Southampton docks to await their fate. They were a sorry sight. Some wag posted a huge sign on the dock fence proclaiming, 'Cunard Bargain Basement Sale'.

One of the first to step up and bid for *Caronia* was a Yugoslavian company intending to use her as a floating hotel in Dubrovnik. However, the sale fell though after it was discovered just how much work the engine room needed.

Not so deterred was the Star Shipping Company, registered in Panama. They completed a purchase deal, renamed her *Columbia* and sailed her to Piraeus to undergo a complete overhaul. Once she arrived, one of the partners, Andrew Konstaninidis, bought out the other Star partners, had second thoughts on her name and painted *Caribia* on the stern. With the green gone and the hull painted white, she began her new cruising career sailing from New York to the Caribbean in February 1969.

Things did not go well. A ship that once offered the extreme luxury of close to one crew member per passenger was now offering something extremely lacking in service. There were numerous passenger complaints, particularly about the waste system. This makes for a very unhappy ship.

On her second cruise, 5 miles out from St Thomas, a steam pipe split open, killing one of the crew, severely scalding another and cutting power to the ship. She drifted for twenty hours while temporary repairs were made. She limped back to New York on what became her last passenger-carrying voyage.

The rest of the cruise itinerary was cancelled, and she was laid up first in Gravesend Bay, off Brooklyn, while the owner tried to deal with legal claims. Chief among them were lawsuits for $1.6 million crew severance pay, and from Cunard pursuing an unpaid $1.5 million payment.

While Andrew Konstaninidis was trying to raise funds to pay off debts and get the ship running again, the insurance company insisted the ship be properly berthed at a pier. Eventually, the ship was moved to an abandoned pier. However, the move was made without the approval of the City of New York, which, in response, issued a parking ticket for the ship.

Faced with parking fines from New York City and numerous litigation claims, it was decided to sell off at auction her interior furnishings and accept an offer of $3.5 million from a scrap-metal shipbreaker in Taiwan.

Sinking on a Bomb

In the spring of 1974, the German Ocean tug *Hamburg* attached *Caribia* to the end of a 3,600ft-long steel cable and towed her ignominiously out of New York for her final voyage to the breaker's yard at Kaohsiung.

After passing through the Panama Canal, they called in at Honolulu to make engine repairs to the tug. But this did not solve all the tug's problems. As they neared their destination, an engine began operating at greatly reduced power, so it was decided to stop at Guam to again make repairs.

However, Tropical Storm Mary rapidly developed before there was time to avoid it. *Hamburg* radioed Guam to say they were having trouble controlling their tow.

Unfortunately, huge swells at the harbour entrance made it impossible for any ship to leave and come to their aid. Left to their fate and driven by wind and current towards rocks at the Guam harbour entrance, the windage of *Caribia* was now doing the towing, dragging the underpowered *Hamburg* with her.

Realising the battle was lost, 900 yards from the harbour entrance, to save his own ship, the captain of *Hamburg* ordered the tow line cut. *Caribia* drifted towards the port's opening. At one stage it looked as though she was going to be blown right into the safety of the harbour, but she hit the inside of the entrance wall with a resounding crash. Waves 40ft high broke against her, breaking her into three pieces. Because of the shallow water she did not sink entirely, but her size effectively prevented any ship from entering or leaving the harbour.

As soon as the storm eased, attempts were made to remove her so the harbour could again become operable. However, they discovered a snag. On the sea bottom, right alongside the *Caribia* was a Korean War landing craft filled with munitions including 5 and 8in unexploded shells.

Fifty tons of ordnance had to be removed first. If *Caribia* had sunk a few feet to the left, she could have gone out with a mighty bang and the demolition job would have been done.

Caronia was one of the finest ships to sail the seas, yet at the young age of 19, she died early. Her painful, lingering death I put squarely at the doors of the British Seamen's Union and their long strike in 1966.

16

SS *Mariposa*
(Later SS *Homeric*)

SS *Mariposa*. (Australian Maritime Museum on The Commons, via Flickr)

Born	1932
Died	1974
GRT	18,017
Length	632ft
Beam	79ft
Passengers	704
Crew	359
Line	Matson Line
Sister ship	SS *Monterey*

Luxury Queen of the Pacific

My ambition to sail the Pacific was burned into my teenage soul by the Rodgers and Hammerstein film *South Pacific*, screened in glorious wide-screen Todd-AO colour at my local cinema. Accustomed to living in cold and comparatively drab England, I sat stunned by the exotic scenes of dense tropical foliage, swaying palm trees, the gold of the sandy beaches, the deep blue of the seas and the majesty of the heat-hazed magical mountains. Most of all, I fell hopelessly for Bloody Mary's hap-hap-happy talking, finger-waving, long-haired and beautiful daughter Liat. 'You like?' No, I love. I had to go there.

I carried this love for many years and in my mind I see her still. My first fiancée had long black hair and an olive complexion. Was I still subconsciously pining for Liat? Probably. The fiancée was not so good at the art of mime, but she did have an entertaining and possibly unique way of being able to make a ladylike burp on request, any time, any place. She was great fun at dinner parties.

First fiancée, I hear you ask? Well, there were a few, but that's the unhappy lot of young men going to sea for long periods and leaving their loved one back in port to wait for them. They don't.

At the time, one of the most popular ways of seeing the South Pacific for real was by a ship from Matson Lines. A friendly travel agent was kind enough to let a young me take home a beautiful colour brochure showing both the ships and locations.

The ship that impressed me most for its romantic ports of call was *Mariposa*. There have been a few *Mariposas*, a fact that seems to have confused some social media marine historians. The one I am talking about was a part of Matson Lines' 'White Fleet', launched in 1931 and first sailed in 1932 from New York.

Her ports of call included a veritable smorgasbord of exotic locations. Through the Caribbean to Havana and the Panama Canal, then on to Los Angeles, San Francisco and other ports on the West Coast, before heading off to Hawaii, Samoa, Fiji, the South Pacific islands, Auckland, Wellington and Sydney. How I yearned to see such faraway places.

Others seemed to agree with me as she had excellent bookings. She also won the hearts of Australians and New Zealanders travelling to Hawaii and the mainland United States.

Mariposa and her two sisters became known for their white hulls, streamlined superstructure, speed, early use of air conditioning and sumptuous interiors. *Mariposa* also had an aft funnel slightly shorter than the one in front. This gave her a very sleek profile. This idea was copied by other ships until the days of the single funnel arrived. *Mariposa* became known as the 'Luxury Speed Queen of the Pacific'.

All this romance and adventure was brought to a sudden end by the arrival of the Second World War. The US War Shipping Administration requisitioned her for troop carrier work and providing supplies to countries on the verge of invasion. But she did not become an official US Army Transport ship.

Returned to Matson Lines in 1946, she was in a very sad state indeed. Matson wanted to restore her and sent her to a shipyard in California to be fixed up. But the cost was astronomical and did not equate with the decreased passenger traffic. It was decided to defer the refit until conditions improved. This went on for six years, until in 1953 Matson gave up and ordered a new *Mariposa* instead.

Second Chance as SS *Homeric*

She was bought by the Italian firm Home Lines. First they repaired her engines in California and then sailed her to Trieste's Monfalcone Shipyard for a modernisation, Italian style. They gave her a more raked bow, enclosed some of the superstructure and fitted her with new cabins with larger square windows.

They took away the aft masts and one funnel and installed a new lido deck with a swimming pool. She was still painted white but with new house colours on the funnel.

The ship's public rooms were given a Greek theme. Cabins were made light and most had private facilities and beds that could be folded into a recess during the day to make a comfortable sofa.

As SS *Homeric*, she was fitted to a standard enabling her to set off in 1955 to compete on Atlantic crossings in summer and Caribbean cruising in winter. Eventually, her popularity turned her on to full-time Caribbean cruising.

Her career came to an unexpected end when in July 1973, a fire broke out in the galley and dining rooms while she was off southern New Jersey.

The fires were contained, but the cruise had to be aborted. The passengers were disembarked and the ship sailed to Genoa.

Again, the damage was so extensive and the cost of repairs so high, Home Lines decided to sell her to the breakers. However, her steam turbines were sold to her sister ship, then sailing as *Britanis* for Chandris Line. So you could say her heart lived on.

17

SS *Nieuw Amsterdam*

SS *Nieuw Amsterdam*. (Author)

Born	1938
Died	1974
GRT	36,667
Length	758ft
Beam	88ft
Passengers	1,220
Crew	694
Line	Holland America Line

The Darling of the Dutch

So far, there have been four *Nieuw Amsterdams*, all belonging to Holland America Line. The first, launched in 1906, was driven by both sails and engines, ironically a concept returning to fashion due to rising fuel costs, environmental concerns and advances in new sail technology.

Next, in 1938, came the true darling of the Dutch and the subject of our story. She was succeeded in 1983 by another, but this one ended up sailing under a variety of names before being scrapped in 2018. Lastly, in 2010 came the largest version sailing today. However, our ship was born and died with the name *Nieuw Amsterdam*.

Why this preoccupation with the name 'Nieuw Amsterdam'? Well, the Dutch, God bless 'em, don't want us to forget it was they who first settled in Manhattan. The colony was granted self-government in 1652 and, as New Amsterdam, was formally incorporated as a city in the following year.

In 1666, the Dutch did the best real-estate deal of all time by purchasing for 60 guilders the whole island they called Manahatta from the Lenape. Incidentally, the official documents make no mention of bonus beads, so it's hard to know where that 'strings of beads' story came from. Sixty guilders has been calculated in today's terms as representing more than $1,000. However, for that today, you would be hard pressed to buy 1sq. ft of Manhattan real estate.

But the British were coming and forcibly took over and renamed the island Manhattan. Nevertheless, 300 years later, the Dutch seek to remind everyone it was their former colony and what better name could you choose for a ship sailing from Rotterdam to New York than *Nieuw Amsterdam*?

So back to our *Nieuw Amsterdam*, which in fact was nearly named *Prinsendam*, but instead, the company decided to cash in on the historical link. By the 1930s, Holland America Line was well established but had been chipping away at the Dutch Government for a bit of a handout to build a running mate for *Statendam*. While other governments, such as the French, English and German, aided the building of ships for either prestige or for the right to allow them to be armed and used as troopships, the more neutrally minded Dutch Government was reluctant to get involved in private enterprise.

In the Netherlands, shipbuilding was in a perilous state, with many of the Dutch orders for new ships going overseas. In the end, the government gave in and made a loan for a new ship, but only on the condition it was built in the country.

She was not to be the biggest on the Atlantic. The design spurned ambition to be the biggest, grandest or fastest. Instead, the Dutch wanted a liner to bolster the local shipbuilding industry and to be seen as a warm and comfortable part of Holland, and a reflection of her people.

For this she adopted the art deco trend of the day, with fabulous and plentiful artworks and warm pastel colours. Elegance was the theme with large public rooms and large staterooms. At the time, she was the biggest ship the Dutch had built and, in 1937, Queen Wilhelmina gave royal approval by turning up to do the launching honours.

Not Caviar Again

When I joined as a ship's photographer in 1963, I found the first-class dining room a very impressive affair with gold leaf columns, ivory walls, tinted mirrors and Murano glass lighting under a Moroccan leather ceiling. There were no portholes because it had been realised that passengers looking out at the sea sliding up and down could be made more prone to seasickness. However, I found watching the soup go up and down in the bowl equally disturbing.

The menu was superb, rich and elaborate in its offerings. But you can have too much of a good thing and eating there every night for a year, I found myself scouring the menu from hors d'oeuvres to cheese board to try to make up a simple meal for my more plebian taste. With the steward's sympathetic help, it was possible to come up with plain dishes, such as fish and chips.

Not so impressive was my allocated tourist-class cabin, which, although roomy enough, was located low down in the very stern and just above the props. As we thundered across the Atlantic at speed, the noise was deafening. My head would vibrate on the pillow like a ball bouncing around on a roulette wheel. However, in the Caribbean cruising season, a more leisurely pace was set that enabled me to fall asleep instead of being knocked unconscious.

Paying passengers enjoyed more salubrious and peaceful accommodation and the ship laid claim to having the highest percentage of cabins with baths of any ship sailing. The theatre was also something special with deep-cushioned seats. Apart from *Normandie*, it was the only dedicated theatre at sea, plus it was air-conditioned. In fact, the air-conditioning plant was the most powerful one afloat.

When launched she had six wide ventilation slots in her first funnel. A slightly odd look but the ambition was that these would give the black sooty smoke that belched from the funnels in ships those days a bit of a lift. The idea was to keep the aft deck clear of falling soot and stop the choking of passengers taking a stroll on desk. However, this was a disaster because they caused a downward draft that made it even worse. So they were promptly welded closed. In the less engine-efficient days of the 1960s, we still had to put up with the same black clouds wafting the decks as was happening on other ships.

She quickly became a favourite with the rich and famous on the trans-atlantic route, but as political tensions built, people from across Europe flocked to the ship to escape the coming horrors of the war. When it finally came, the Netherlands, a neutral country, quickly painted in large white letters along the hull her name and her country for correct identification.

However, even for ships from neutral countries, the North Atlantic was not a safe place. So she opted for the safer passage of taking people on cruises from New York to the Caribbean. As she was to prove for many years after, with her air conditioning and her smaller size, she was well suited to this task.

In May 1940, the Germans took the Dutch by surprise by invading the neutral country. The Netherlands did fight back, even going to the extent of flooding the central part of her low-lying land. However, after a relentless bombing campaign, she eventually succumbed to occupation. For certain fear of falling into enemy hands, *Nieuw Amsterdam* could not return. Instead, she was converted into a troopship, given a lick of war-time grey camouflage paint and armed with thirty-six guns. Her speed gave her a good chance to outrun both U-boats and their torpedoes. Thus equipped and under the management of Cunard White Star, she began carrying British and North American troops to North Africa and the Pacific theatre.

Most of her original crew complement stayed with the ship through both the Caribbean cruising and her war service. They were away from home for more than six years. Her contribution to the war effort was substantial as during her secondment she carried more than 378,000 troops and travelled more than 529,000 miles. The Netherlands was, rightly, very proud of their ship. She became known as the 'Darling of the Dutch'.

In May 1945, she returned to her builders to strip out the troopship adaptions and adorn her once again with her fine artworks and luxurious fittings for a return to North Atlantic passenger service.

Troops being transported to the theatres of war can be hard on a ship and often, as a rite of passage, took to carving their initials into any wood they could find, along with such illuminating messages as 'Kilroy was here'. Nobody seems too sure what this meme means, but my favourite theory is that Kilroy was thought by Hitler to be an Allied spy and the troops did it in fun and with the thought of unsettling Hitler. Maybe it drove him mad. Something did.

When she arrived home, battered and war worn, to an equally battered and war-worn Rotterdam, huge crowds gathered ashore and on boats to give her a rapturous welcome. For the Dutch, her return signified the war was finally over.

The refit and repairs to her cost more than her original build, but now resplendent in her Holland America Line colours, in 1947 she resumed her peacetime transatlantic schedule. The stars and the celebrities came back, along with masses of business folk and holiday travellers. Not only was the ship popular, but she was also very profitable on the North Atlantic run.

In 1956, *Nieuw Amsterdam* was sent for a major refit to install stabilisers and be given a general upgrade to keep her in tip-top condition. Many passengers were reluctant to cross the North Atlantic at its winter worst, so ships were increasingly taking to cruising from New York to the Caribbean during the winter season. Accordingly, Holland America Line opted for a new paint scheme and replaced the traditional black with a light grey colour to keep her cool in tropical waters. It was a very classy look.

Such was the success, Holland America introduced a running mate, *Rotterdam*. Now there was *Statendam*, *Rotterdam*, *Prinsendam* and, as we crew members liked to say, '… all the other dam ships!'

But they were all very happy ships. The Dutch were sticklers for cleanliness and good order, but on cruising, crew dress-up parties were legendary. At the time, there was a craze going where everyone was trying to create new records on how many people could be squeezed into a small space, such as a telephone box or a Mini. And so it was with our parties.

A typical crew party. The author is the little face peeping out the back row, fourth from right. (Author)

There always seemed to be an all-out bid to cram as many crew into a single cabin as possible. Being squashed up against each other in outlandish dress and with hardly room to breathe certainly created an atmosphere of informal intimacy.

We would amuse ourselves by raucously singing disgustingly filthy sea shanties, of which there seemed an endless supply. And always someone at the party, whatever their nationality, could and would recite the entire poem 'Eskimo Nell'. Oh yes, we were a classy lot.

This photo (above) was taken on either my eighteenth or nineteenth birthday. I don't remember. My party was given a Halloween theme and people poured into our cabin. One officer, who shall be nameless, arrived through the porthole. To do this, he would have had to have been lowered on a rope from the cabin above, all while steaming across the Atlantic in the middle of the night.

You could always tell when things were getting a bit too raucous because some of the more senior officers would begin to discretely disappear. This party ended with an overly dramatic finale. The heat from all our crushed together bodies and the heavily smoke-laden atmosphere triggered the automatic fire sprinkler system, completely drenching us all.

Initial screams quickly died down and a whispered evacuation happened with incredible speed. Everyone tried to get clear before the alarm on the bridge sent a fire crew with a senior officer to start taking names for punitive action.

At this stage, the party was judged to have been a complete success.

Once, ashore in St Thomas, I discovered a duty-free liquor store selling a huge whisky bottle mounted on a miniature replica of a golf buggy, complete with wheels. The golf buggy might have been a miniature, but the bottle certainly wasn't. It contained around 5 litres. I had to have it.

I staggered back to the ship and proudly propped it in a corner, ready for the next crew party. Unfortunately, a couple of nights later, the ship developed a bit of a roll and both whisky and cart took off across the floor to smash into the other side of the cabin. I think it was the only time I cried on that ship.

The crew also had a variety of hidden talents and were happy to put on a special crew show for the delight and surprise of passengers. They might discover the Dutch East Indies waitress in the dining room could perform a talented and wonderful candle dance; the wine waiter could sing with a fine tenor voice and even us photographers from England, swinging walking sticks and dressed up in red-striped jackets, white flannels and straw boaters, linked arms, barber shop quartet style, to belt out with bad aplomb, 'Oh, it's a lovely day to be beside the seaside'. And for an encore, 'Hello, hello, who's your lady friend'. My singing voice is terrible, but maybe it was my first step to becoming an entertainment officer on board *Queen Mary*.

When the airlines began moving the transatlantic liners' cheese in the mid-1960s, more and more ships turned to Caribbean cruising. *Nieuw Amsterdam* was one of the best equipped to make this transition, but, when her boilers packed in, it looked like her days were numbered.

It was now 1967, and at this stage, most ships with such a big problem went to the breakers. But Holland America Line searched the world and managed to discover some replacement boilers. So instead of scrapping her, the Dutch cut a gaping great hole in the hull and installed replacement boilers. This was major surgery indeed, but with a new lease of life, she gave up the transatlantic and went for the easier life of cruising the Caribbean from Port Everglades.

But her time came, and in 1974, she began her last voyage. This was to the Taiwan breakers. There had been the usual outcry to save the ship and convert her to a hotel in Rotterdam. But few ships make this transition successfully.

However, *Nieuw Amsterdam* had a long and illustrious career, and it is only fitting that today her name is still proudly carried on by the Holland America Line.

18

SS *Angelina Lauro*
(Formerly MS *Oranje*)

SS *Angelina Lauro*.

Born	1939
Died	1979
GRT	24,377
Length	672ft
Beam	83.6ft
Passengers	1,230
Crew	290
Line	Flotta Lauro

Disaster at St Thomas

For forty years, this humble ship made a significant impact on the lives of around a million people across the world.

Slightly too early to be a war baby, she was christened in 1939 by the Netherlands' Queen Wilhelmina as *Oranje*, in honour of the Royal House of Orange. The launch did not go well. After the queen pulled the release lever, the ship stood motionless on the slipway for an hour. Commented the queen, 'She is a real member of the House of Orange, we are all quite rigid.'

Orange was the adopted colour of the royal family and to this day still adorns the Dutch football team. Distant forebears aside and accepting there was a strong republican move to distance itself from the House of Orange, it is hard to understand why they would name a ship *Oranje* as the Netherlands had ditched the colour orange from the striped national flag in 1660. They altered it over time by slowly progressing the orange to a deep red. It is all a bit double Dutch.

National identity confusion can arise at sea now as both the Netherlands and France have red, white and blue stripes. The only difference is the Netherlands' stripes are horizontal and France's are vertical. Flapping about on the stern of a ship, or hanging down in windless conditions, can cause momentary muddles, but the Dutch will be quick to tell you they were first to adopt this tricolour.

The Dutch can also lay claim to being the first country in the world to produce a motor liner able to reach a maximum speed of 26.5 knots. This was partly attributable to another first in the unusual amount of tumble-home shape in *Oranje*'s hull.

Tumblehome is not a late return from the pub, but a term describing a hull that grows narrower above the waterline than at its beam. The reason to adopt it was to give the ship less draft, enabling visits to shallower ports of the Dutch East Indies. It also minimised Suez Canal transit charges.

The opposite of tumblehome is flare, and this is usually markedly noticeable in the bow. It is shaped this way to break through the seas. In the case of *Oranje*, the tumblehome made her 17ft wider at the top of the hull than at the waterline. So, the eye could not miss it and, if anything, it made her womanlier. The only drawback was it made the ship inclined to roll a bit more in a sea.

She was outfitted with a first class for 283 passengers, a second class for 283 passengers, a third class for 95 and, wait for it, a fourth class of 52.

In my days of travelling the Atlantic, I don't think any of the ships were still offering fourth-class travel. These cabins were dormitory style and crammed into the very end of the stern and low on the waterline. The noise and vibration of the engines was both deafening and bone shattering. I suspect I may have travelled in one that had undergone the luxury of a conversion to third. My head literally bounced up and down on my pillow all the way across the Atlantic.

On other ships, I had cabins crammed into the forward part of the ship. Engine noise was not a problem here, but when the seas rose rough, they would thunder against the hull. Sleeping with ear plugs and going up and down in an express elevator could bring on a bout of seasickness for even the hardiest of sailors.

Worst of all was when the ship dropped anchor. The noise of the chain rattling though the hawser was deafening and the whole cabin would shake like a jolted jelly. If you're prone to seasickness, the best place to be is in the middle of the ship on the lower decks.

Going to War

Oranje entered service in June 1939 in competition with *Willem Ruys* (see the separate story on *Achille Lauro* in Chapter 21) on a regular run to the exotic islands of the Dutch East Indies. She was soon to stay there for more than a year when, at the start of the Second World War, she was laid up in the Indonesian city of Surabaya.

But she was not to escape war duty. At the expense of the Dutch Government, in early 1941 she sailed to Sydney for conversion to a hospital ship.

She was painted entirely white, save for a wide green band around her hull and huge red crosses on her sides and funnel. This was in the hope that any U-boats or air attackers would be commanded by gentlemen. It was no guarantee. During the war, twenty-four hospital ships were sunk by everything from torpedos to enemy aircraft.

Nevertheless, now under Australian naval command, but with a Dutch crew and a Dutch flag still fluttering on her stern, the *Oranje* set sail to her first theatre of war. Over the next five years she made forty-one voyages to theatres of war in the Pacific, Asia, Middle East and North Africa. She cared for more than 32,000 wounded Australian, New Zealand and British soldiers and escaped unscathed from any attacks.

With the war over, in 1946 Australians crowded the Sydney headlands to give her a grateful send-off. On her first voyage home, she could not reach Amsterdam itself due to the bomb damage done to the locks. When she finally made it, the Dutch gave her a rapturous welcome. Then she was off to the dockyard to spend six months being refitted once more as a gracious liner.

She resumed her regular pre-war service from Amsterdam to the Dutch East Indies in 1947. On one trip in 1953 the smooth routine was interrupted by a head-on collision in the middle of the Red Sea with her rival ship, *Willem Ruys*. She was travelling the same route but in the opposite direction. This was no glancing bruise, the bows were badly damaged and while buoyancy wasn't affected, both ships needed repairs.

How on earth could this happen? Well, it was common in those days for ships to pass each other as closely as possible. This exciting manoeuvre was made to relieve the passengers and crews from the monotonous boredom of long days of sailing empty seas.

Surprisingly, there were no long confrontations in court. Instead, peaceful negotiations ended in the two rival companies merging. The Dutch can be very pragmatic. In the merger, *Willem Ruys*, *Oranje* and *Johan Van Olden Barneveldt* joined forces to become the Royal Dutch Mail.

Meanwhile, the locals in the Dutch East Indies were coming a bit restless of life as an occupied territory. The Dutch had first arrived in 1596 but during the war worse was to come. In 1940 Germany, Hungary, Italy and Japan got together to divide up the world, and the Dutch East Indies fell into Japan's sphere.

The Netherlands, the USA and Britain tried unsuccessfully to defend the colony as the Japanese moved south in quest of Dutch oil fields and rubber plantations. At first, the local population welcomed the Japanese as liberators. Then they discovered they were more oppressed than before. The UN reported that Japanese occupation cost 4 million dead.

After the war ended, the Dutch tried to resume affairs but by then guerrilla groups had formed to fight for an independent Indonesia. In December 1949, the Netherlands formally recognised Indonesian sovereignty and now the old colonial ties were broken, new routes needed to be found for *Oranje* and her sister ships.

Oranje was given another wash and brush up, with fourth class being abandoned in favour of extending the deck space aft and installing a cinema amidships. She now travelled between Amsterdam, Southampton, Suez, Singapore, Australia and then New Zealand. She came back home via the Panama Canal, stopping at Port Everglades and Bermuda before returning to Southampton and Amsterdam.

However, she was fighting a losing battle with the airlines, so the company experimented with a few European cruises, which failed financially, and it was finally decided to put her up for sale.

Sold to the Italians

Both her, and her fellow ship, *Wilhelm Ruys*, were bought by Flotta Lauro. Signor Lauro named *Wilhelm Ruys* as *Achille Lauro* after himself and *Oranje* was named *Angelina Lauro*. When I worked on *Achille Lauro* there were all sorts of rumours as to who Angelina was. I never found out which was true.

All traces of being *Oranje* were erased at Italy's Cantieri del Tirreno shipyards. The ship was lengthened by 16ft by introducing a long, sweeping bow and the promenade deck was both extended and enclosed with glass. The funnel was modernised by adorning the top with distinctive smoke-deflecting wings and the interiors were given the Italian décor treatment. Completion of the conversion was delayed when a fire broke out on board, which resulted in the death of six people.

In 1966 she finally emerged as *Angelina Lauro*, flaunting all the grace and style for which Italy is renowned. Her mission, for the next six years, was to join *Achille Lauro* carrying migrants from northern Europe and the Mediterranean to new lives in Australia and New Zealand.

By 1972, migrants were switching to air travel and Flotta Lauro decided it was more profitable to revamp her into a one-class ship and send her cruising. She proved successful in this role, but Flotta Lauro wanted to relieve itself of the marketing of the ship and in 1977 chartered her out for a three-year stint with Costa Lines.

Costa contented itself with merely painting its house yellow colour on the funnel, adorning it with the usual large letter 'C' and shortening her name to *Angelina*. She operated out of Port Everglades and Puerto Rico and gained great popularity on the Caribbean cruise circuit.

However, in 1979 tragedy struck while she was moored at the dock at Charlotte Amalie on the island of St Thomas. Fortunately, the passengers were mainly ashore including, less fortunately, many of the fire-trained crew.

In the aft crew galley, a fire broke out and it spread rapidly forward through the restaurants and into the passenger cabins. If there had been more crew about, the fire could possibly have been contained, but it soon spread through to the top decks.

Shore fire crews and harbour fire boats arrived and began pouring water onto the outbreak. This must be done to put a fire out but at the same time it went to prove how nothing had been learned about fighting fires in dock since *Normandie* rolled over in New York Harbor in 1942.

Sure enough, the fire water poured on the upper decks pooled on one side and *Angelina* began to list. To stop the possibility of any fire spreading to the dock and not wanting it filled with a sunken ship, attempts were made to tow her away. But by then she was too heavy with water and touching the bottom, so couldn't be moved.

Marine fire expert Tom Guldner* advises to simultaneously begin removing or relocating fire water and giving priority to the upper decks as there it has the maximum leverage on the degree of tilt. It should be a case of one litre in and one litre out. He advises that if the pumps are unable to pump overboard, then the water should be pumped down into the ship's bilge, where it can either be pumped out or, with monitoring, can remain at this safer, lower area.

Guldner says one trick is to quickly send water to lower levels by breaking toilets in any flooded upper-level areas. This will allow the water to drain into the ship's sanitary tanks in the lower levels of the ship. Alas, none of this was done and *Angelina* listed and sank at the dock.

Passengers, dressed in shorts and tee-shirts, arrived at *Angelina* to find their ship in flames and lying on her side. Their clothing, their passports and all their other possessions were beyond their reach.

---

* Tom Guldner is a retired lieutenant of the New York City Fire Department's Marine Division who also held a US Coast Guard licence as a ship's master. He is a participating member of the Society of Naval Architects and Marine Engineers (SNAME) Fishing Vessel Operations and Safety panel and also their Small Working Vessel Operations and Safety panel. Tom is also a Principal Member of the NFPA Technical Committee on Merchant Vessels. His articles on marine firefighting have been published both nationally and internationally and can be found on his website www.marinefirefighting.com.

Other ships in port came to the rescue and took on the homeless passengers. *Sun Princess* was able to take on 400 of them, feed them, take them to Puerto Rico and help arrange for flights home.

Much to the distress of the port of Charlotte Amalie, *Angelina* was deemed a total loss and remained sunk at their dock for three months. It took a long time to find a salvage crew, but eventually they were able to pump out her water and refloat her, tow her away from the dock and off to Taiwan for the scrapper's graveyard.

It was to be a slow death. They managed to get her through the Panama Canal but, when she was in the middle of the Pacific, her weakened hull began to take on water. She remained afloat for three days, listing and sinking ever lower. Finally, not two weeks after her fortieth birthday, the proud ship once known as *Angelina Lauro* rolled over and sank.

19

SS *Admiral Nakhimov*
(Formerly SS *Berlin*)

Last day of steamship SS *Admiral Nakhimov* in the port of Novorossiysk before the disaster on 31 August 1986. (AndreasJonke CC BY-SA 4.0, via WikimediaCommons)

Born	1925
Died	1986
GRT	17,053
Length	572ft
Beam	69ft
Passengers	1,125
Crew	354
Line	Black Sea Steamship Company

Disaster for the Russians

What a fascinating and varied life this ship led. Built in Germany for North German Lloyd, she began her career as a transatlantic liner on the Bremen to New York run in 1925 as SS *Berlin*. She was the third passenger ship to bear this name, but she was the only one to be abandoned by the Germans and later 'found' by the Russians. A case of finders keepers.

She had given Germany loyal service, mainly operating on the Atlantic. She was first in the news in 1928, when she was one of the rescuers racing to the aid of the British-operated passenger ship *Vestris*.

Reportedly, *Vestris* left New York for Buenos Aires in an unseamanlike state with coal heaped on top of the bunker hatches that had not been battened down. She was heavily overloaded and floating below her hull markings. Not a good way to go to sea.

On her second day out, she ran into a storm, which shifted both her cargo and bunker coal. This caused the ship to list and huge seas swept the decks and flooded below faster than the bilge pumps could cope with. The captain was forced to give the order to abandon ship, but she succumbed to the fierce sea before all lifeboats could be launched.

She sank off the coast of Virginia with the captain and others still on board. Many of the survivors were picked up by SS *Berlin*, but 113 could not be saved.

Free Cruises for All the Workers

The war clouds were gathering and in 1939 the Nazis chartered SS *Berlin* for propaganda purposes. After all, she had the right name and, in letting her go, it is unlikely the shipping company had much choice in the matter.

What would the Nazis want with a passenger ship? Well, the idea was to use her as part of their 'Strength Through Joy' programme, known in German as NC *Gemeinschaft Kraft durch Freude* (KdF).

Following the Nazi suppression of the unions, they were keen to prove what good chaps they really were and set out to prove it by offering near free cruises to the workers. This move to lower the divide between the haves and the have-nots was supplemented by other goodies. These included bringing down the price of the coveted motor car so low that ownership was within reach of everyone. Thus, the Volkswagen Beetle was born. Such offerings were a very effective inducement to join the Nazi Party. Quickly, the KdF became the world's largest tourism operator.

When the inevitable war finally began, that was the end of the subsidised cruises for workers' lark and instead she became a hospital ship able to accommodate 400 patients. And just to make it clear, she was now sailing under the catchy identity of *Field Post Number 07520*. She was sent to serve in Norwegian waters.

Towards the end of the war, she was assigned to Operation Hannibal, a mission to transport soldiers and refugees back home from the Eastern Baltic. All did not go well in 1945. While she was forming up to join a convoy, she struck a mine, disabling her propellers. But she was still afloat and set off under tow to the port of Kiel. However, on the way she struck yet another mine. This time her hull was so damaged, she was in danger of sinking completely. She was quickly towed into shallow water and beached.

Passengers were offloaded, much to their relief no doubt. The Germans did salvage as much equipment on board as they could, but eventually left the stricken hull to meet the fates of nature. But it was not to be nature, it was the Russians.

Four years later, the Russians came along, inspected the hull and claimed marine salvage rights. They made some repairs, refloated her and had a free cruise ship.

They named her *Admiral Nakhimov*, in honour of a Russian naval commander during the Crimean War. She began in 1957, operating as a peaceful passenger ship cruising the Black Sea between Odessa and Batumi. Carrying around 1,000 passengers, the Russians had got themselves a bargain.

She was briefly called up again during the 1962 Cuban Missile crisis to carry troops to Cuba but when that stand-off petered out, she returned to her passenger service.

'Alive and Well in Novorossiysk'

The years went relatively peacefully until early one night in 1986 she set off on a cruise with 346 crew and 888 mostly Ukrainian passengers. She had just left the Black Sea port of Novorossiysk, on the south Russian coast, when she noticed approaching on the portside an 18,000-ton Russian freighter carrying oats and barley.

A warning was radioed to the freighter, but the reply said they would make sure to pass clear. With that, the captain of the *Admiral Nakhimov* left the ship's bridge to his officers and went to bed.

However, the captain of the freighter neither changed his speed or course. He ploughed on.

At 11 p.m., *Admiral Nakhimov* called several times on the VHF radio asking for their course. No answer. At 11.10 p.m. they altered their own course correctly to port and seconds later called the freighter to demand it immediately reverse full astern. But it was too late and two minutes later the freighter ploughed at 5 knots into the cruise ship's side, smashing a gaping 900sq. ft hole through the hull between the engine and boiler rooms.

Admiral Nakhimov immediately listed, and as there was no air conditioning and ninety of the ship's portholes had been propped open, water literally flooded in everywhere. Passengers and crew were forced to find their way in darkness to the open decks and then, fearful at how fast the ship was sinking, jumped into the oil-slicked sea. There was no time to launch lifeboats and within seven minutes she went straight to the bottom.

This all happened just 8 miles from the port and helicopters and rescue ships were quickly on the scene. They managed to pull 836 people from the oily water.

Those in the sea were so slimy with oil, many sailors from the rescue ships had to jump in to help the survivors be pulled out. Their hands and arms were so slippery, they could neither hold on to dropped ropes or outstretched arms.

Although 423 of *Admiral Nakhimov*'s passengers perished, there were no fatalities on board the freighter. At the following inquiry both captains were found guilty of criminal negligence and sentenced to fifteen years in prison. *Admiral Nakhimov*'s captain received his sentence because it was considered he left the bridge at a time of potential crisis.

The Soviets like to control their news media and news of the disaster was withheld for forty-eight hours. Survivors were prevented from transmitting messages to their loved ones other than, 'Alive and well in Novorossiysk'.

20

SS *America*

(Later USS *West Point*, SS *Australis*, SS *Italis*, SS *Noga*, SS *Alferdoss* and SS *American Star*)

SS *America*. (Author)

Born	1940
Died	1993
GRT	26,454
Length	723ft
Beam	93ft
Passengers	2,258
Crew	643
Line	United States Lines

'There She Is, Miss America'

Having once sailed with the great songwriter Bernie Wayne, I suspect when writing his famous song, 'There She Is, Miss America', he was thinking of something a little curvier and slimmer than this ship with a beam of 93ft. Certainly, the Miss America pageant made no such connection when adopting it as their theme tune. They have nothing approaching 26,000 tons on their catwalk.

But the ship herself was a real beauty and attracted great American pride as the nation's flagship. However, even after the most loyal service, national pride can often prove rather fickle. In her prime she was sold off to masquerade under the name of *Australia* and then *Italy*, before finally being brought back for a brief and very ignominious period as *American Star*.

It does seem a bit odd to see a nation's flagship eventually sold off to another country and then bearing the new country's name. Now she's mine, now she's yours. A bit like divorce. She was bound to come to a sad end. In the preservation stakes, her transatlantic running mate, SS *United States*, only did a little better. Although, as you will see in Chapter 32, even that claim is questionable.

However, SS *America* was off to a very glamorous start, built in the United States and launched in the pre-war gloom of 1939 by the liberated and outspoken Eleanor Roosevelt. As a Roosevelt, Eleanor was well connected before marriage: she became even better so as the wife of the President of the United States.

By 1940, the final touches had been made and SS *America* was all set to fly the Stars and Stripes across the Atlantic for America. But this run was short-lived. The very next year, while happily idling around the Caribbean, she was called both up and back for conversion to a troopship.

The navy, for some reason, maybe to ensure she was well and truly branded as one of their own, renamed her USS *West Point*: perhaps slightly less patriotic, but with more of a military ring. In this role she was a real trooper. In fact, she carried more than 359,000 of them. In 1946, she was handed back to United States Lines and once again named SS *America*.

In 1952 SS *United States* arrived as her transatlantic running mate. The new ship was longer, sleeker and faster and snatched the role of being the country's favourite. The travelling public can be so fickle. In comparative terms, *America*'s reign was relatively short.

However, she had her faithful followers who found her more homely and cosy than her somewhat austere and sterile running mate. In the winter season, she would cruise the warmer and gentler waters of the Caribbean. Besides, rather than face a stormy Atlantic crossing, transatlantic travellers were showing a distinct preference to fly.

Of course, when times are challenging and the going gets tough, shipping unions, for some completely unfathomably reason, take this into their heads as being the ideal time to fight for better wages. They did not believe the company's protestations about losing money and went on strike for more pay. This drove a stake through *America*'s fluttering heart and saw her laid up Hoboken for five months with nowhere to go.

She was never to sail as a US-registered ship again. In 1964 she was sold to the Greek-owned Chandris Line, which faced none of the union challenges besetting American and British companies.

I do not wish to be too hard on the shipping unions, as in the early days they did much to put to rights the shocking lot suffered under some owners. However, more recently shipping unions seem to be cursed with some sort of self-destructive death wish. While they may set out with the desire to increase the prosperity of their own seamen, it always seem to turn out mainly to create opportunities for crews coming from Eastern Europe and the Philippines. In a sense, this is good: it helps spread increased prosperity across the world.

Going Greek

Certainly, the Greeks had a use for her and put her on the Europe to South Pacific run to serve the migrant-starved country of Australia. They didn't rename her as *Australia*, but *Australis*: not because the Greeks can't spell, just because they liked their migrant ship names to end in 'is', such as: *Ellinis*, *Patris* and *Britanis*. You get the idea. There was even an *Amerikanis*, which would have been an ideal fit, but alas, that idea didn't have its eureka moment until three years later.

Chandris liked to 'pack 'em in'. They added an extra 350 cabins and increased the number of berths in the existing cabins. This took passenger capacity from 1,200 to 2,258. Ka-ching!

She began service in her new role in 1965, but after the closure of the Suez Canal in 1967, she skipped calling at the now diversionary course to

Piraeus, and instead sailed the enforced longer route around the tip of South Africa to reach Australia.

A fire broke out in the galley in 1970, but the crew managed to contain the blaze, and after some repair work was done, she continued her voyage. So, fire at sea is not always fatal.

In 1974, *Australis*, while in Sydney Harbour, was involved in a minor collision with HMAS *Melbourne*. This was a dangerous ship to pick a bingle with as *Melbourne* was an aircraft carrier of the Royal Australian Navy. While never having fired a shot in anger, she had managed to sink two Allied ships and was now becoming considered accident prone. Fortunately, in this harbour incident, although both ships suffered some damage, there were no casualties.

Mutiny

Come 1977, *Australis* was the last regular ship left on the migrant run. Australia finally decided it was full up. *Australis* was laid up for a year in New Zealand before being sold back to an American company, Venture Cruise Lines, in New York. They promptly renamed her *America* but were not sufficiently patriotically moved to exchange her registration from Greece to the more expensive and restrictive requirements of the US. Thus, she avoided falling once more into the hands of the US unions. She was given a facelift with the hull painted dark blue and the two funnels tricked out in patriotic blue and red. She looked the real deal, but alas, her beauty was all on the outside.

When she opted to keep the schedule of her first cruise in 1978, the ship was in a terrible mess. Boarding passengers encountered piles of rubbish, soiled linen, worn mattresses and repellent smells. Overhead, pipes were leaking and dripping fearful-looking liquids onto the decks. On top of that, the ship was heavily overbooked.

She had only just got past the Statue of Liberty when a group of passengers mutinied and sought their own liberty by forcing the captain to return to the pier and let them off. On docking, 960 passengers fled.

Undeterred, later that day, with considerably fewer passengers, SS *America* set off again. But everything was still in such a state that in the time it took to reach Staten Island in New York Harbor, another 200 loudly complaining passengers were taken off by the Staten Island Ferry.

The captain was determined to sail on. However, her arrival in Nova Scotia was not a triumphant affair. Instead, she was met with writs and legal claims from passengers coming to $2.5 million.

Thus, this turned out to be the first and last cruise the renovated SS *America* was to make. The public health service moved in, gave her a score of six out of 100 and ordered her to be sold to cover her overdue debts.

Guess who bought her? Why, Chandris of course. For only $1 million, they bought her back. Of course, the company had to spend more returning her to a usable condition. Her forward funnel was rusted through, but, as it was only a dummy, it was removed entirely. It modernised her silhouette and in 1979 she was ready for work.

Chandris christened her *Italis* and sent her off to be a hotel ship for a conference in Liberia, before putting her on a short season of Mediterranean cruises. Even so, Chandris was worried about getting their money back and opted to sell her to a group called the Intercommerce Corporation. They immediately renamed her *Noga*. This was most likely the Hebrew meaning of splendour, or morning light. A bit ironic as the plan was to convert her to be used as a prison in Beirut.

But even there they have standards for prisons and evidently, she was not up to the criteria. After four years of rusting away idle, she was sold to Silver Moon Ferries, which half-named her *Alferdoss*, which is Arabic for paradise.

I say half-named, as *Alferdoss* was painted on the dockside port bow only. On the other side of the bow and stern it still said *Noga*.

But did they really care? Not too much, as before she even sailed a burst pipe flooded the engine room and cabins and it was decided the best thing to do was to sell her for scrap. A company offered $2 million, made a deposit of $1 million, demolished some lifeboats and davits, defaulted on further payments and pulled out.

Was this the end? Not quite. In dry dock, the weary old lady revealed a handsome hull still in good condition and was thus sold in 1992 to be refitted as a five-star hotel ship off Phuket.

She would have to be towed there. This time she was renamed as *American Star* and a year later set off for a 100-day tow to start a new life in Thailand.

On the journey, in a thunderstorm in the North Atlantic, the tow line snapped. Attempts to reattach one were unsuccessful. They did manage to get six people aboard the ship and two other tugboats were called to assist.

But in the wildly pitching seas it was difficult enough to stand up without trying to deal with reconnecting thick tow lines. A helicopter came and retrieved the crew from the ship, and she was left abandoned to drift at the whim of wind and waves.

She ended up on the rocks on the coast of the Canary Islands and within forty-eight hours had broken in two. So, far beyond salvage, after fifty-five years' service, on 6 July 1994 she died. Left to the mercy of nature's slow erosion, only at a very low tide can some signs of the wreckage of this once great liner still be seen.

21

MS *Achille Lauro*
(Formerly MS *William Ruys*)

MS *Achille Lauro*.

Born	1947
Died	1994
GRT	23,629
Length	642ft
Beam	82ft
Passengers	1,372
Crew	300
Line	Flotta Lauro Line

Fires, Collisions and Hijack

Maiden voyages, I try to avoid. In fact, I've only ever done two: once in a flight of fancy on *QM2*. And the other was the maiden trip of *Achille Lauro*. As I had worked on the last crossing of *QM1*, to my mind it made some form of connection to be thirty-seven years later on the first voyage of *QM2*.

On maiden voyages you get enthusiastic receptions in all the ports: all the hoopla of fire boats spouting coloured water, marching bands and quayside dancing. On the other hand, there are countless tales of anything but plain sailing: long waits in the dining room, flooding in cabins, electrical failures and tendering and boarding processes that take forever. It takes a little time to properly shake down a ship and you cannot iron out all the wrinkles of running a full load of passengers on the first trip.

So, in my capacity of being the photo unit manager on board the maiden voyage of *Achille Lauro*, I arrived a week early and was determined there would be no teething problems in my department. We did get everything shipshape and working well. However, on the fourth day sewage erupted out of the pipes in the darkroom. I was not amused. Nor was the clean-up crew.

But was this really a maiden voyage? This was 1965 but the ship had been built as *Willem Ruys* and had been sailing for Rotterdamsche Lloyd for eighteen years. However, the Italian shipyard had done an amazing conversion job, transforming her from a traditional style to a sparkly, amazing-looking modern liner.

As *Willem Ruys* she had a chequered career. The keel was laid in 1939, but work ceased as the fledgling ship hunkered down to avoid Second World War bombing raids. She emerged unscathed amidst the intensely bombed surroundings of shipyard buildings.

However, as a reprisal against sabotage elsewhere by the Dutch resistance, the Nazis took the founder of Rotterdamsche Lloyd, Willem Ruys, hostage. This was an attempt to make the saboteurs surrender. They didn't. So, the Nazis shot him. After the war, in his honour, the company named the new ship after him.

Wilhelm Ruys, the ship, began life carrying migrants from the Netherlands to the Dutch East Indies. On that route, while crossing the

Red Sea, she collided in broad daylight, slap-bang, head-on with her main rival, *Oranje* of the Netherlands Line. You can read more about this collision on page 139. As a result of subsequent merger negotiations, *Willem Ruys*, *Oranje* and *Johan Van Olden Barneveldt* joined forces to become the Royal Dutch Mail.

When the Dutch East Indies colonies were handed over to local governments, traffic on the route dramatically declined and thus the ships were diverted to the Americas route. But with continuing declining traffic, *Wilhelm Ruys* was sold to the Italian Flotta Lauro Line and renamed *Achille Lauro*, again after the owner. A decision, we assume, few company employees would dare to query.

She emerged completely rebuilt and exhibiting all the flair of Italian design. This time, no world war interrupted the progress, but an explosive fire on board caused a major delay to her completion.

Shot at the Quayside

We set sail on our maiden voyage in 1966, picking up migrant passengers from Germany, France, Scandinavia, the Netherlands and Belgium and then on to pick up even more nationalities in Southampton, Genoa, Naples, Messina, Valletta, Beirut, Port Said, Suez and Aden.

Then, with this very disparate assortment of nationals, we set off in sweltering conditions on the long journey across the Indian Ocean. Migrants were dropped off in Fremantle, Melbourne and Sydney before terminating in Wellington, New Zealand. Then this thirty-four-day route was reversed, picking up young Aussies and Kiwis off on their adventure pilgrimages to Europe.

There was a vast difference between the two legs of the voyage. On the way over, the hotchpotch of nationalities often didn't get on at all well. Grudges from the Second World War and the fights in Cyprus and Egypt lingered on in many minds. And the mix of religions and politics added fuel to the flames. It seems adherents to the main gods have zero tolerance towards the beliefs of others. Portia got it wrong. The quality of mercy is very strained.

Some of the dockside scenes in the Middle East would see migrants trying to sell their last possessions around the foot of the gangway. A few sheep and goats were popular items on offer. Huge crowds would gather, and the dealing and bargaining would lead to much shouting and a few scuffles.

Once, when leaning over the ship's rail in Beirut, watching a riot on the quay, I saw a policeman draw his gun and shoot a man in the shoulder at point-blank range. The man staggered backwards, fell between the ship and the quay and the water turned red.

The long days of hot passage from Aden to West Australia, with no whiff of land, inflamed some migrants to the extent it sometimes even made crossing the crowded purser's square hazardous. Occasional knife fights broke out and the burly crew of the master at arms was kept busy breaking up melees and putting people in the brig.

I remember standing with the young Australian education officer watching some on-board chaos erupt. It was her job to travel on board to give lectures and prepare the mix of nationalities for life in Australia.

I asked her if Australia knew what it was doing? Most had no knowledge of English and the Australian way of living. She replied that it was not them Australia wanted. What Australia wanted was their children. And indeed, Australia was proved right, for the arrival of the migrants has greatly enhanced the nation's culture.

The run back to Europe was vastly different. Here were the young, off on their first trip overseas to see their motherlands, determined to have fun and revelling in the discovery that the price of beer on board was nearly a quarter of that ashore. Cut-price beer? See how life on ships has changed!

Later runs down to Australia became more settled, particularly when *Achille Lauro* brought back to England the British servicemen caught up in the unrest in Aden. Their presence seemed to discourage wild breakouts on board.

The crew, however, were fun and we had heaps of good times. I was reluctant to leave. For a bit of company I had two pet goldfish in my cabin. They had voyaged with me from Southampton to New Zealand and back a couple of times. Not a bad swim for a couple of goldfish and we had formed a bit of a bond.

When I was transferred to another ship, I wanted to take them with me, but I wasn't too sure how I was going to get a bowl of goldfish past customs in England. Surely, they had a couple of laws forbidding that.

The two ship's nurses said they had an idea. On arrival in Southampton, they dressed up in their full nurse's uniforms and put the goldfish bowl on a metal tray along with a pair of forceps. They then covered the bowl with a white cloth, lightly dabbed with tomato sauce.

Down the gangway they marched, side by side urgently and intently, straight through the customs hall. They attracted a few official glances, but no customs official was game enough to step forward, stop them and see what was under that blood-stained cloth.

Achille Lauro continued without me, but political unrest was everywhere. It was one of the last passenger ships to complete a northbound transit through the Suez Canal before the Six-Day War closed and blockaded it for eight long years.

I wonder what happened to the cheating Gully Gully men who used to surround ships in the canal in their boats, laden to the gunwales with fake carpets, jewellery and souvenir camels stuffed with used bandages. They were expert at amusing talk while switching goods, performing magic tricks and swindling.

Achille seemed accident prone. In the process of being converted to a cruise ship in 1972, she again caught fire. Three years later, she was in yet another collision and sank the cargo ship *Youseff*. She suffered another big fire in 1981. But a far worse one was to come.

Hijacked at Sea

With the migrant trade declining, a year later Lauro Lines went into bankruptcy and the ship was leased on charter to Chandris Line. But her luck was not to change and in 1985 she was highjacked by the Palestine Liberation Front (PLF).

In Genoa, 748 passengers embarked on a Mediterranean cruise that included ports in Egypt and Israel. Among them, posing as Argentinians, were the four PLF terrorists.

After docking in Alexandria, most passengers set off on a bus tour of the pyramids. They were very lucky. The plan was for the group to move on to Port Said, where they would re-join the ship fourteen hours later.

According to passenger reports, while the ship was still docked in Alexandria, a camera crew arrived to film a fictional scene of people running on and off the ship firing blank guns. This was later thought to be a ruse to confuse everyone while real guns were being smuggled aboard.

With the near-empty ship now under sail to Port Said, a steward delivering a fruit bowl surprised the four terrorists in their cabin cleaning their guns. The original plan was to begin the hijacking when the ship reached Israel. But realising they were now discovered, they burst into a panicked reaction and immediately stormed the dining room, where most of the passengers left on board were having their meal. They entered, firing automatic guns over their heads. The sight, sound and splintering of glass set people screaming and falling to the floor. Some tried to escape through the kitchens but were mercilessly chased down and brought back.

A report of the shootings reached the bridge and the captain set off to investigate, but he was urgently called back to be confronted by a terrorist with a machine gun. He was told there were twenty armed terrorists on board and he should order his crew to stand well clear of the ninety-seven remaining passengers who had not gone on the pyramids trip. If anyone were to approach, they warned, they would start killing the hostages.

He was ordered to set course for Syria. Only later did the captain learn there were only four terrorists. However, the bridge did manage to get a distress call out before the hijackers remembered to order radio silence.

Back in the dining room, two women passengers were given a hand grenade each and told to keep the release lever firmly gripped. The detonating pins were pulled out. If the women were to relax their grip, the hand grenades would explode. As night fell, the hostages were taken up to the promenade deck lounge and given blankets to settle down and attempt sleep. Containers filled with gasoline were placed around the lounge and the crew were warned if they attempted rescue, they would be set alight.

Meanwhile, the 651 passengers on the pyramids trip arrived in Port Said to find no ship waiting. Initially there were complaints, but after they were finally told what was happening, they realised how lucky they were.

Achille was to spend the next two days at sea with the hijackers in control. Via radio they demanded the release of fifty terrorists imprisoned in Israel. They had ordered the ship to Syria, but the Syrians wanted no part of it and refused entry.

The hijackers then did the unforgivable. To show they had no mercy, they picked out a Jewish, wheelchair-bound passenger, Leon Klinghoffer. While he was still sitting in his wheelchair, they shot him dead. Then, they inhumanly tossed both his body and chair into the sea.

As governments became aware that *Achille Lauro* passengers were being held hostage, the immediate outrage resulted in a horrendous political farce. Leon, along with some other passengers, were American citizens. Accordingly, President Reagan readied a team of SEAL commandos from Delta Force and Air Force combat controllers from Brand X. This was not a washing powder, but the name for a section of the Air Force Special Tactics Combat Rescue team. Italy sent sixty paratroopers and four helicopters, and all assembled at a British-owned NATO base on Cyprus. They were not to work together.

The Americans, with the idea of keeping the ship in international waters, asked all countries along the Mediterranean shoreline to deny *Achille Lauro* access to their ports. This was followed by a political bun fight between the main protagonists: Italy, Palestine, Egypt, Syria, Tunisia, Jordan and the USA. It became the beginning of the 'Sigonella Crisis'.

The mastermind of the attack, Abul Abbas, safely ashore in Palestine, realised the situation was way off plan and out of control. He sent a message to the four terrorists that the ship should go to Port Said in Egypt, where in return for not harming passengers, they would be given safe conduct.

While several countries were pursuing claims to prosecute the terrorists in their country, Egypt wanted no part of it. However, they did allow the ship to dock and for the terrorists to be exported on an Egyptian civilian plane to Tunisia. There, the four were to be tried by the PLO.

Thinking this would mean no justice would be served, the United States Air Force intercepted the plane and, flying wingtip to wingtip, threatened to shoot it down if it did not divert to Sigonella, an airport in Italy that also had a US Navy facility.

On landing, the plane was surrounded by eighty US troops, but they in turn were soon surrounded by a massive force of armed Italians. The SEAL team went aboard to find the four terrorists and their commander Abbas surrounded by ten Egyptian commandoes and an Egyptian ambassador.

The Egyptians were not happy. Nor were the Italians. There was a major dispute about who had the right to arrest the terrorists. The Italians insisted they had territorial rights over the base, the hijackers and the Egyptian plane. The Egyptians claimed they had diplomatic immunity and should be free to leave, and pointed out they held jurisdiction over *Achille Lauro* as she was berthed in Port Said. Finally, to save shooting breaking out, it was agreed Italy should have the hijackers and release the plane and Egypt would release *Achille Lauro*.

The Italians took the hijackers to court. Sentences ranged from fifteen to thirty years, but the paroles were extremely liberal and given early. Two hijackers disappeared while on parole. A third was sentenced to thirty years, but was later released on parole. He too, escaped. The fourth, the one who shot Leon Klinghoffer, was sentenced to thirty years, but after ten years was given a ten-day furlough. Of course, he escaped.

Initially the Italians resisted attempts for mastermind Abbas to be handed over to the US for trial. They claimed there was insufficient evidence for a conviction. While they were still arguing, Abbas vanished. However, the Italians did sentence him to life imprisonment *in absentia*.

During the Iraq War, the Americans finally caught up with Abbas and took him into custody. The Pentagon reported that he had died of natural causes just under a year later.

Life as Star Lauro

Four years after the hijacking, *Achille Lauro* was taken over by the Mediterranean Shipping Company and was renamed *Star Lauro*. But in 1994, en route to South Africa, a major fire broke out while she was off the coast of Somalia. On board was a total complement of 979 passengers and crew.

Italian officials first blamed the fire on a passenger's discarded cigarette. At sea this has always been one of the main concerns. A carelessly tossed cigarette over the side can be fanned by the breeze and blown through an open porthole below to start a fire.

In this case, it was utter nonsense as what really happened was one of the boilers exploded and caused an electrical fault. It went undetected for some time and thus the fire was able to take a firm hold. This is hard to understand, as although the engines were old, in the modernisation project an air-conditioned control room was installed with large soundproof glass windows looking out over the engines.

In my time on board *Achille Lauro* this was always manned. It was kept immaculately, save for a dirty oily rag hanging over the end of a brass rail. When I asked what on earth that was doing there, the chief laughed and said it was to remind him of how life was in earlier days when he had to be right inside the hot, noisy engine rooms to check everything over.

But that night the fire raged out of control undetected. A Mayday was sent just before five in the morning, but the shore base did not relay the distress call to all shipping until an hour later.

Video taken by those on board and posted online shows the smoke billowing from the funnels getting darker and darker as the minutes ticked on. It also shows buckets of water being hoisted laboriously aboard. This was as practical as trying to fill a bath with a teaspoon. However, lifejacketed passengers were assembling, and lifeboats were being prepared for launching.

Later footage shows flames leaping from the side of the ship and the fire taking firm hold on both the fore and aft decks. Mercifully, the sea was serene. As was cruise staff member Moss Hills, who calmly directed passengers to the lifeboats. After all, he was experienced at this: three years before, as you can read in the chapter on *Costa Concordia*, Moss was a hero and one of the last off the ship. This time he had a better captain, who was among the very last to leave.

You may have thought that after two sinkings, Moss would review his career choice. In fact, he went on to become a cruise director for many more years at sea.

The videos of the passengers and crew in their life jackets waiting for their boats to be lowered show some grim faces, but in the main everyone seems in good spirits. All the passengers were got away and the lifeboats were taken aboard a tanker, two bulk carriers and USS *Halyburton*.

The fire burnt for two days before finally being extinguished by the sure way of the ship slipping gently beneath the waves.

Amazingly, the only causalities were two people who died of heart attacks and only eight people were injured.

But it was the end of a magnificent ship.

22

MS *Estonia*

(Formerly MS *Viking Sally*, MS *Silja Star* and MS *Wasa King*)

MS *Estonia*.

Born	1980
Died	1994
GRT	15,598
Length	510ft
Beam	79ft
Passengers	2,000
Crew	180
Line	Estline

Mystery of a Modern Ship Disaster

One of the strongest superstitions of the sea is that it's bad luck to change a ship's name. Said Long John Silver, 'What a ship was christened, so let her stay.'

Stories abound of ships, renamed in a moment of folly, meeting sudden, tragic, watery ends. Legend has it that when a ship is christened, its name goes into the great Ledger of the Deep. This is maintained meticulously by none other than the bearded, gym-fit, trident-wielding, budgie-smuggling King Neptune himself. You can't slip anything past that god of the deep.

During her fourteen years, this ship was named four times and she sank with the horrific loss of 852 lives. Recently, some thirty years later, a new board of investigation was tasked to examine the true cause of this deadliest peacetime sinking of a ship in European waters. For a peacetime sinking at sea, it is second only to *Titanic*.

In the years since, there have been numerous rumours and a new investigation hopes to solve them. Was it caused by stormy seas? Was it the fault of poor design and maintenance? Or an explosion of clandestine munitions smuggled aboard? Or was it a collision with a Russian submarine? Was it a planned terrorist attack? And what happened to the Russian captain? Why were suggestions to raise the ship to answer these questions squashed? Was the original inquiry suppressed by governments? What did they have to hide?

New technology is likely to discover the truth by using a super-sensitive, camera-armed robot to be lowered 265ft to carefully examine every aspect of the sunken *Estonia*. Their mission has been helped by a slight shifting of the ship since the diver survey for the previous board of inquiry.

One undeniable fact has quickly emerged. The rip in the bottom of the *Estonia* is far bigger than first thought. Significantly, one of the holes burst the steel hull out and not in, as would happen if the sinking was caused by a reef or a collision with a submarine. Only a massive internal explosion could have caused that.

Unfortunately, the exploring robot's photography excursions on the seabed came to a sudden halt when it got jammed between the hull and the bottom of the sea. Officials are trying to stop further exploration and are sticking to the finding that the bow visor was faulty in construction.

Murder at Sea

Estonia began life as a proud member of Viking Line and was called *Viking Sally*, a name English people might find not too friendly for a visitor to their shores. But her run was well away from East Anglia and went from Stockholm to Mariehamn, an island port of Finland, and then on to Turku on the Finnish mainland. She was half cruise ship and half car ferry. She had nine decks and could accommodate 2,000 passengers and 460 cars.

Constructed in the German shipyard of Meyer Werft, she had a bow that yawned up and open to swallow cars and lorries onto her lower decks. Vehicles were said to roll on and roll off and this type of ship is referred to as a RORO.

Looking at the record, one may conclude travelling by cruise ship/ferry is not the safest thing to do. In July 1986, while en route to Stockholm, a businessman's cabin was invaded by two men, who robbed the occupant of his wallet. When the businessman said he was going to the police, the main assailant stabbed him five times in the throat with a dinner knife and then, with the assistance of his accomplice, strangled him to death with a strip of fabric torn from the cabin's bedsheet.

The assailant was found guilty and sentenced to life imprisonment. Two years later, he escaped with two other inmates, shooting a prison guard in the arm with a sawn-off shotgun. He then took to robbing banks with his fellow escapees but settled a division of the spoils dispute by killing one of the men with an axe.

Now recognised as one of Finland's most dangerous criminals, he was caught and returned to jail. He was pardoned by the Finnish president in 2004, only to be back before the courts in 2011 on a new charge of manslaughter.

A year after that attack on *Estonia*, in July 1987, two young West German tourists, in their early twenties, were travelling together and chose to save on an optional cabin. After a convivial time in the bar with newfound friends, they first bunked down in the saloon. But they found it too crowded and thought they might be better off on the open deck. The decision cost Klaus Schelkle his life and his girlfriend, Bettina Taxis, was seriously injured.

At 1.00 a.m., they gathered up their sleeping bags and took them to a sheltered, dimly lit spot on the top deck. Just before 4.00 a.m., a wandering group of three Danish scouts discovered the couple barely conscious, reeling and bleeding from horrific wounds. It appeared the pair had been attacked with one of the ship's emergency axes fixed about the upper deck.

The ship's nurse persuaded the captain to order an immediate helicopter to fly them to the hospital at Turku, where the ship was to arrive later that morning. Klaus was pronounced dead on arrival. Bettina survived but had no memory of what happened.

Before the ship docked in Turku in the morning, police and crisis scene investigators arrived aboard by helicopter. They started off interviewing the 1,400 passengers, but there were too many for the police to handle.

There was no available CCTV footage of the area and eventually even the selected possible suspects had to be let go. However, two months later, some fishermen discovered a bag of clothing on an uninhabited islet just 200m from the ship's sea lane route. Thinking nothing of it at the time, they left it there, but a year later they went back and discovered the bag still there. This time they took it with them and gave it to the police.

They discovered clothes from the ship and found it contained a glove monogrammed with the letters 'H.K.'. The police continued interviewing former passengers and kept the case open while forensic science continued to make strides.

Although initially the police had been looking to place a charge of manslaughter on a suspect, they felt they had insufficient evidence. With the case still open, twenty years after the crime took place, advances in DNA technology gave them the evidence they needed. But by then it had passed that crime's statute of limitations.

However, the police charged a Danish suspect with murder, which has no statute of limitations. The man, who was one of the former boy scouts first on the crime scene, had allegedly confessed to the crime and described the murder weapon used. However, he recanted when the murder charge was made to beat the statute of limitations provision.

The court ruled that as the guilty statement had been taken without a lawyer or other independent witness present, that evidence could not be presented to the court. He was therefore acquitted. At the time of writing, the case was waiting on a high court appeal.

Challenging King Neptune

While all this was going on in the law courts, the ship became involved in a corporate tangle. Her ownership became a confusing jumble of associated companies. She was operated in 1990 by Siljan, named *Siljan Star* and repainted in their colours but kept the same route. A year later she went through another corporate shuffle and was renamed *Wasa King*.

The following year her name changed yet again. She became *Estonia* and was chartered by a company registered in both Cyprus and, following the collapse of the Soviet Union, the newly independent Estonia.

The Baltic is a very busy shipping area, and it remained so in the darkness of night on 28 September 1994. The wind was gusting at 34–45mph and the waves were rising to highs of 6m. It was a rough night.

However, it was nothing unusual for the Baltic at that time of year and all the usual ferries were operating as normal. *Estonia* was late departing the Estonian port of Tallinn but left at 7.15 p.m., keen to arrive in Stockholm at her scheduled time of 9 a.m. the next day.

She was carrying 803 passengers and 186 crew on board. The vehicles and cargo could have been better distributed, and she was wearing a slight list. Once at sea, it seems she was travelling just a couple of knots below her normal speed, which most experts agree was too fast for the conditions at the time.

Around 1 a.m., there was a loud metallic bang, thought to be caused by a big wave hitting the bow doors. The bow, or stem of the ship, is the wave-breaking part of the hull and must be very strong indeed. However, *Estonia*'s bow could be opened like the jaws of a crocodile, with the top part hinging open to allow vehicles to drive into the ship. Such a design is called a visor bow and when properly engineered it should not be weaker than a normal bow.

With the visor bow door broken open, the sea flooded into the open car deck and, as it did, the water tried to level out. However, as the ship rolled, all the water rushed across the deck to the lower side and its weight prevented the ship from righting. Listing at this precarious angle only caused more water to flood in. This is known as the Free Water Effect and can very quickly induce a ship into a death roll.

As soon as the water poured in, the ship listed 15° to starboard. Five minutes later, a quiet voice announced an alarm and then the crew and passenger emergency sirens blared out.

Passengers and crew were scrambling from their cabins, but water was flooding through everywhere. Some cabin doors could not be opened due to the pressure of the water in the outside corridor. Adding to the torrent, big waves were smashing through cabin windows and into the public rooms.

A typical bow visor for loading vehicles onto a ship. (Wolfgang Hägele, WikimediaCommons, CC A SA 3.0)

Within minutes the ship listed 60°. A distress call was made, but not in the proper manner, which cost valuable time. Also, there was a delay in getting an exact position out. At 1.50 a.m. *Estonia* completely disappeared from other ships' radar screens.

Despite there being approximately 2,000 ships in the Baltic, due to the poor Mayday call and the fact it was made to a sister ship and not a proper 'all ships call', the ferry, *Mariella*, the first of four vessels to respond, did not arrive for another twenty-two minutes.

The unfortunate thing was that when *Mariella* relayed the message, the wireless operator opened with the less urgent pan-pan signal, rather than the proper one, which is 'Mayday' repeated three times. A full-scale emergency was declared at 2.30 a.m., nearly an hour later, which was a catastrophic delay for the hundreds of people in the very cold water.

Swedish and Finnish rescue helicopters arrived at 3.05 a.m. By then around a third of those who escaped *Estonia* had died of hypothermia. The subsequent commission of inquiry estimated that up to 310 passengers reached the outer decks. This means 679 people were inside the ship. Only 160 managed to board life rafts or lifeboats. With a water temperature of 10°C, those in the water had little chance of survival.

Ship Burial at Sea

In the investigation that followed, the failure of the visor was blamed. While there is the factor of possible poor maintenance, a French court said the shipyard was not responsible for any major structural defects. After all, she had made numerous crossings of the Baltic in such conditions.

The investigation also said *Estonia* should have immediately slowed down after hearing the first bang, but the bow visor was not visible from the bridge. The officers were further criticised for the delay in sounding the alarm and not following proper Mayday procedures.

There was a move to have the ship raised to determine the true cause of the sinking and to recover bodies for proper burial. However, many felt the bodies would have decayed to the extent that they were better left where they were. Instead, the Swedish Government suggested taking the unusual step of encasing the hull in a shell of concrete.

Thousands of tons of pebbles were dropped on the wreck and in 1995 a treaty between Sweden, Finland, Estonia, Latvia, Poland, Denmark, Russia and the United Kingdom was signed to prohibit their citizens from approaching the wreck. The wreck's security is monitored by the Finnish Navy.

These moves to keep everyone away only added fuel to the flames that the authorities had something to hide. In 2019 a Swedish film crew defied the ban and hired a German ship to take them to the wreck site to make underwater explorations. They discovered a 4m hole in the ship's hull that could not have been made since the ship sank.

This find did not stop the Swedish documentary makers being prosecuted for violating the wreck, but they were acquitted in 2021 when it was pointed out that Germany had not been a signatory to the sanctity agreement, and it was a German survey ship in international waters. But in 2022, a retrial found the two men guilty and both were fined.

The broadcast of the documentary forced the Estonian, Swedish and Finnish governments in 2021 to announce a new investigation, with a former Estonian state investigator into the sinking saying he believed the hole was most likely caused by a collision with a submarine. The results of this inquiry were released in 2023, but this report concluded the same as the original 1997 inquiry and provided no new evidence to contradict it, continuing to blame the bow visor locking mechanism.

Explorations have continued and have revealed more holes, the biggest being about 22m long and 4m high. This most significant hole is one where the metal is bent outwards, which many claim could only have been caused by an internal explosion.

In 2004, a former Swedish customs officer claimed *Estonia* had been used to transport military equipment, leading to speculation that the cause of the visor door coming off could have been the result of an explosion. The Swedish and Estonian governments, forced to launch separate investigations, confirmed non-explosive military equipment was on board the ship. The Swedish Ministry of Defence said no such equipment was on board. Go figure.

There is no doubt that the loss of the bow visor caused the ship to sink. But why exactly did it fail? Time will no doubt reveal the full truth, but that might not be for decades. As for the rumours that the ship's captain was seen ashore after his presumed death, it is more likely he went down with his ship.

23

SS *Canberra*

SS *Canberra*. Evening departure from Sydney to Auckland. (Author)

Born	1961
Died	1997
GRT	45,720
Length	818ft
Beam	102ft
Passengers	2,188 first class
Crew	900
Line	P&O Orient Lines

Taking Passengers Down Under

Today it is unspeakable, but strange as it might seem, SS *Canberra* came into being as a direct result of the White Australia Policy. This blight on Australian history was officially enacted into law in 1901. It was one of the first pieces of legislation brought in by the newly formed Federal Government of Australia.

Said the Attorney General, Alfred Deakin:

This puts in plain and unequivocal terms the prohibition of all alien coloured immigration, and more, it means at the earliest time, by reasonable and just means, the deportation or reduction of the number of aliens now in our midst. The two things go hand in hand and are the necessary complement of a single policy – the policy of securing a 'White Australia'.

What a start to the new federation! And this was decades before Hitler began talking of his vision for a 'master race'.

The problem was the local population of predominantly British settlers were none too happy about the influx of non-white migrants. They were lured by cagey settlers to the gold rush as an alternative to paying 'proper' wages to white employees.

As the flows from the rivers of gold dried up, many of the migrants moved to the city and went into business in competition with the white settlers. This led to some of the Australian states going as far as excluding anyone of non-British descent. They considered non-whites to be morally and intellectually inferior and the indigenous Australians to be a 'dying race'.

Asian people particularly felt the brunt of the whites' apprehensions, and this was only fortified by Australia's encounters with the Japanese in the Second World War. By the late 1940s, only 2.7 per cent of the population was not of Australian, Irish or British descent. The Asian population had shrunk to less than a quarter of 1 per cent.

I hasten to point out this is a far cry from the Australia of today, a very multicultural society, with those of Asian descent greatly enriching life in the country. But back then, with millions of Asian people living on their doorstep, the comparatively small group of white people in Australia were fearful of what was termed a 'Yellow Peril' invasion. The mantra for white people was 'populate or perish'.

Accordingly, the Australians introduced an Assisted Migration Scheme to lure people from war-ravaged and food-rationed Britain to a grand life in the land of plenty, perpetual sun, golden sands and 'schooner'-sized beer glasses. The cost of this epic cruise across the globe? Just ten British pounds. In today's money that's around £435 – still a very reasonable price for a five-week cruise across the world.

The catch was you had to take a health check and promise to stay in Australia for two years. If you went home earlier, you had to fork out around £120. Most stayed. They became known as 'Ten Pound Poms' – a term rarely hinting at the faintest whiff of endearment. Children were carried free, but teenagers could travel for £5.

In my later teens and living in Britain, I raised the five quid and put in my application. However, as an asthmatic, I failed the health check. But years later, when I was in Hawaii, I jumped onto *Oronsay*, one of *Canberra*'s sister ships, and hopped over to Australia under my own steam. So far, they have let me stay. I guess I am what they call 'one of those boat people'.

Come the Second World War, to help protect Britain, Australia loyally sent thousands of its own men to die in the muddy battlefields of Europe. With the war finally finished, it was realised the depleted population of both countries was putting strong restrictions on the number of available migrants. In between 1945 and 1972, more than a million migrants arrived from the British Isles. But it was not enough. The net had to be increased to take in all of Europe, up to and including Lebanon. After all, they all wore white skins.

Consequently, the demand for migrant ships was strong. Australia was a long, costly flight away. The Australian migrant trade was dominated by two British shipping companies: P&O and Shaw Saville. However, once the selection of migrants was opened across Europe, other country's shipping companies began to compete for a share of the action.

It was in this atmosphere that the need for a British super liner was recognised by P&O. At a time when in their board rooms shipping companies were throwing conniptions at the looming threat of air travel, P&O, revelling in migrant commissions from the Australian Government, was emboldened to order what was thought to be the last great ocean liner to be built.

The wife of the Australian prime minister, Dame Pattie Menzies, launched the long white liner with her distinctive and proud aft set side by side funnels from the Belfast slipways of Harland & Wolfe in 1961. It was a tour de force for the shipping company's PR. Get the wife of the biggest customer to launch the ship and name her after the Australian capital. Fittingly enough, Canberra is the Aboriginal name for 'water'.

Canberra was designed to carry 538 first-class passengers in salubrious surroundings and 1,650 tourist-class passengers in tiered bunks, a queue for the toilets and a fight for the laundry. In those days, unlike the airlines of today, the nobs sat more amidships, and poorer mortals were either crammed into riding the ups and downs of the bow or bouncing at the other end of the seesaw at the very back of the stern. Being right aft has the bonus feature of engine noise plus manic, thunderous vibration. In this area, as a crew member on another ship, my head on my pillow would bounce up and down like a ball in an air lottery machine all the way from Southampton to New York. Five days across the Atlantic is one thing. Five weeks to Australia is another.

I often worked on foreign-flagged passenger ships, but whenever I spied *Canberra* in a foreign port, I would talk my way aboard for a bit of a look round and to chat with some of her crew. This would inevitably lead to a visit to one of the on-board bars for some good old English Whitbread beer poured straight from the tap, a bit of a sought-after rarity on distant shores. I found *Canberra* to be a wonderful blend of English and Australian décor, obviously designed to make the passengers feel at home as they made their way to a new life in a new world.

During the migrant run to Australia, there were formal nights, when passengers showed up for dinner in their Sunday best and made the ship a little piece of England at sea. Abandoning your country of birth, your friends from school, your relatives, your home and, indeed, everything you know to sail off to the other side of the world to start a new life is a traumatic experience. Dwelling on this in the weeks it takes to get to your new country causes many a passenger to form a strong bond with the ship carrying them on this most important journey of their life.

For this reason, millions of people formed a significant connection to *Canberra*. This only grew when *Canberra*'s migrant runs and world cruises were rudely interrupted by British Prime Minister Margaret Thatcher's desire to send her off to the Falklands War.

For this fight, the lady had no hesitation in seizing Britain's two biggest and grandest passenger ships of the time, *QE2* and *Canberra*. She had them converted to common troopships and sent off as a part of the invasion force into a bloody face-off with Argentina. *Canberra* was then affectionately nicknamed the 'Great White Whale', a possible tipping of the hat to *Queen Mary*'s battleship-grey war moniker of the Grey Ghost.

Over this far-flung, near-deserted island group, lives were lost and ships were sunk. It was an enormous risk to take with Britain's finest ships, but *Canberra* made it safely through the war to resume her peacetime activities.

However, she was not to survive strangulation by the soaring cost of oil and ever stricter safety regulations. After thirty-six years' service to Britain and Australia, it was decided to euthanise the grand lady. In 1997 she was dispatched, along with the hearts of thousands of her loyal admirers, to the breakers' yards for her steel to be recycled.

You never know, when you get in your car for a spin, you just might be driving a little bit of the once mighty *Canberra*.

24

MV *Aurelia*

(Formerly MS *Huascaran* and MS *Beaverbrae* and later MS *Romanza* and MS *Romantica*)

MV *Aurelia*. (Author)

Before as MS *Huascaran*.

Born	1939
Died	1999
GRT	610,480
Length	487ft
Beam	60ft
Passengers	1,124
Crew	182
Line	Cogedar Line

From Caterpillar to Butterfly

She began life as *Huascaran*. As a passenger/cargo ship, she was your traditional, common-or-garden caterpillar. But ten years later, she underwent a transformation. After a few months of Italian shipyard hammering and welding, she emerged from her chrysalis as a beautiful gleaming white butterfly of a cruise ship.

I was assigned to her for a spell of Scandinavian North Cape cruising. She had just finished a term serving as a classroom at sea for students. Serious in their studies they may have been, but I can't begin to imagine what students at sea on a cruise ship got up to once class was over.

I watched the laughing, chattering teenagers clattering down the gangways with their suitcases before I could board to sign on. After, I was back at the gangway to see the arrival of the new passengers for my cruise. They were a much older lot, with serious faces, bald heads, walking sticks and wheelchairs. No wild party material here. As a young bloke, I couldn't help wishing I had been on board for the trips before.

It was just another example of the varied life the ship led. When she first entered service in 1939, she was a very capable German freighter, built for the Hamburg to West Coast of South America run and able to offer luxurious accommodation for fifty-eight passengers.

This was once a popular form of travel. It provided an alternative for passengers who liked long days both at sea and in port: a different experience from the usual hustle and bustle of typical cruise ship fare.

For the Second World War, she was taken over by the German Navy to be adapted and stationed in Norway as a repair and service station for their U-boats. With the war over, she was seized by the British as a war prize and sent to Liverpool for a refit. She was then handed over to Canada for a couple of years of regular cargo work.

She was next sold to Canadian Pacific, which considered the relative merits of using her as a cargo, or as a passenger ship. This dilemma was solved when the company decided to do both. Little was done to change the look of the ship. The company merely added a stack more lifeboats and stuck the Canadian Pacific logo on her funnel.

However, down below, they added extra cabins to accommodate seventy-four passengers and the name *Huascaran* was painted over with MS *Beaverbrae*.

In 1948, she made her first trip with few passengers and holds full of cargo to be unloaded at London's Tilbury Dock. Once the holds were emptied, workmen moved in and, while the ship sailed on to Bremerhaven, converted the hold space into temporary dormitory accommodation for 700 migrants and refugees to make the return trip to Canada.

In those days, ships had first, cabin, tourist and steerage classes. I don't know what you call putting passengers into the holds. Maybe it was stowaway class? In my years at sea, I was allocated a range of cabins of varying quality, but I'm glad I never had to travel in that one. Still, if you're a desperate refugee, it's one way to get to escape to a new land.

By 1954, after carrying 38,000 from Europe to Canada, she was running out of fresh supplies of people and the time had come to seek new pastures. The Italian Cogedar line bought her and set about making a silk purse out of a sow's ear. The Italians are good at that and gave the middle-aged lady the glamour makeover to end all makeovers.

First, she was stretched to have a finer, longer body. This involved sawing her in half at the tummy button, adding a bit in and then sewing her up again. She was given a new superstructure, fitted with covered decks, outdoor pool, sports deck and air-conditioned, comfortable cabins for between two and eight berths. She was then sent to be based at Genoa.

Born Again

In 1959, wearing her new wardrobe, she became the celebrated MV *Aurelia*, ready to attract the more sophisticated migrants of the day for the run to the bottom corner of the globe and start new lives in Australia and New Zealand. She would start her voyage at Bremerhaven, picking up passengers from northern Europe, the Mediterranean and the Red Sea before heading for the lands Down Under.

In the late 1960s, again the winds of change blew across her bows. The airlines were proving cheaper and the number of migrants needed for Australia was dwindling.

Driving a nail into the coffin of the migrant run was the 1967 closure of the Suez Canal by petulant Egyptian President Nasser. Alarmed by the Six-Day War and Israel using the canal to access the Red Sea, he hoped to use the closure to force the international community to intervene. When he closed it, he made sure it was well and truly closed. He blocked it with scuttled ships and floating mines and said, 'Take that' to the West.

The canal remained shut for eight long years, forcing *Aurelia* and all other ships crossing from Europe to the east to make the long and expensive detour around the southernmost tip of South Africa. After a year of making this extended voyage, Cogedar decided that in terms of both time and money they should prepare *Aurelia* for European cruising. This proved far more costly than was budgeted for and took far longer to complete. Several advertised voyages from Southampton to Madeira had to be cancelled, sullying *Aurelia*'s reputation and plunging Cogedar into financial turmoil. While the ship was in Madeira, she was seized, arrested for debt and a forced sale was made to the Greek-owned Chandris Line.

Taken to the shipyards at Piraeus, her public areas were remodelled and more cabins fitted with private facilities. This reduced her passenger capacity to 650, which allowed for some lifeboats to be removed and thus increased her deck areas.

Nearly a year later she emerged, again looking a sparkling brand-new ship. Now named MS *Romanza*, she immediately became popular on the Mediterranean cruise market. From time to time Chandris would lease her out to other cruise operators. After one of these went broke, she joined another company operating out of Brazil and then even for a time cruised the Indian Ocean from a base in South Africa.

During an Aegean cruise in 1979, she ran aground and was so severely damaged and flooded at the bow that she had to offload her passengers and be towed to a shipyard for repairs. After that it was all plain sailing, with the summer Mediterranean season managed by Chandris Cruises, and by independent operators for the off season in South America and the Caribbean,

However, success brought its own problem as the company wanted to replace her with a bigger vessel. So, with the ship in tip-top condition, in 1991 she was sold to a Cypriot company trading as New Ambassador Leisure Cruises.

The Paradise Cruise from Hell

Now named MS *Romantica*, she spent the next four years sailing short cruises from Limassol to Egypt and Israel. It became a popular cruise and after four years faced such fierce competition from other ships, the company was forced into bankruptcy. *Romantica* was laid up for two years.

In 1997, she was off again on Mediterranean cruising, this time with another Cypriot company called Paradise Tours. But it was far from paradise. It was more like hell. After just a few months of operation a fire broke out in the engine room.

A fire at sea is one of the most feared events on a cruise ship. However, this one started early in the morning in calm waters. She was en route to Egypt and still within 70 miles of Cyprus.

The fire spread quickly and established a firm hold. A Mayday distress signal was sent and answered by the former Chandris ship *Princesa Victoria*, another former ship of mine, and we can read her story in the chapter on MV *Victoria*.

In half an hour, *Princesa Victoria* came steaming to the rescue, keen to save her former sister ship. She found 482 passengers and 182 crew already in the lifeboats. They were safely taken aboard with many in their pyjamas and without money or passports.

Helicopters from a British base in Cyprus arrived to directly winch up from the burning ship the last of the crew and the captain. He was able to report the evacuation had gone smoothly with all passengers and crew saved.

Tugs came out to pour water on the flames. It took four days to extinguish the blaze, and, by that time, this once very proud ship was a sad, burnt-out wreck.

She was very well-built and had served her owners with loyalty and dignity across the world for an astounding fifty-eight years. This is a very long life for a cruise ship. *Aurelia* was even able to complete her final voyage to Egypt. Sadly, this was under tow to the breaker's yard.

25

MS *Victoria*

(Formerly MS *Dunnottar Castle* and later MS *The Victoria* and MS *Princesa Victoria*)

MS *Victoria*. (Author)

Born	1936
Died	2004
GRT	15,007
Length	540ft
Beam	72ft
Passengers	600
Crew	250
Line	Incres Line
Sister ship	*Dunvegan Castle*

Crew Idiosyncrasies

Before we begin the tale of *Victoria*, there's something I must confess. I've been feeling guilty for sixty years, so it's time to get it off my chest. I owe a long overdue apology to the hundreds, probably thousands, who sat with puzzled faces in the movie theatre on board the Italian MS *Victoria* cruise ship in the early 1960s.

The only excuse I can offer is I had just began working in my newly promoted position as manager of the on-board photo unit and I was yet to reach 20 years old. Head office in London must have been unable to find anyone else. But I wanted to stun them with my organisational talents.

My new duties included acting as the movie projectionist for the ship's beautiful movie theatre. I had not done it before, but the Italians thought that as I was a photographer, I should be able to handle the ship's movies. They were wrong. The two jobs bear no resemblance.

The films came in giant 35mm reels and to show a movie required the operation of two massive film projectors. Each reel lasts around twenty minutes. So, an average length movie would come in six or seven reels.

To show the movie, you threaded the first reel through a series of cogged wheels on the projector and then repeated this procedure with the next reel on the second projector. Starting the film was easy: you set the projector going with your hand over the lens so the audience couldn't see all those odd numbers and flashes at the start. The moment the sound burst forth and the opening title appeared, you smartly withdrew your hand and the picture appeared on the big screen in all its magic.

To make for a seamless switch from one reel to another, the projectionist carefully watches for a small momentary flash in the top right-hand corner of the screen. This signals time to start the second projector. Standing between the two projectors, you carefully watch for a second flash and the moment you see it, with one hand you throw a leaver to close the light shutter on the first projector and simultaneously with the other hand open the light shutter of the second projector.

With the second reel now safely running, the first reel is taken off and rewound for the next showing and the third reel threaded up for the next change. Got it? Now you know how to be a movie projectionist, that is if you can find a movie projection system from the last century.

If my memory was right, the first film I had to show was *Charade*, starring Audrey Hepburn and Cary Grant. On ships we used to get pre-release films to ensure no passenger had seen it. It was a much-hyped murder mystery, and it certainly attracted enough passengers to fill the theatre.

To enter, everybody walked past the projection booth, and I could hear all their chattering as they entered the theatre. Seconds before the movie started and the lights dimmed, in a blaze of tropical whites and gold braid in came the Italian captain, chief engineer, chief purser, chief steward, ship's doctor and a couple of other senior officers. They took up a standing position in a row at the back of the theatre. Wow. It was my first day in a new job. I'd better not mess up. But I did.

Somewhere between the second and fourth reel, I got distracted. I did the change, turned around and found a reel just sitting on the bench. To my horror I realised I'd left out the third reel. What should I do? Pop it on so it would come up in the wrong sequence or leave it out entirely and get it right the next time. I figured it was a whodunit anyway and a little added mystery wouldn't hurt much. So, I left it out.

As the film ended with twenty minutes of the action missing, the sea of white officers was the first out the doors. I shrunk back, but they hurried off in different directions. As the audience came wandering out, I caught snatches of conversation, 'Isn't Audrey Hepburn wonderful? 'Yes,' agreed another, 'I must get my hair cut like that.' Another was musing, 'I didn't quite get it, how did they know he was the murderer?' 'Really?' comes a superior voice. 'It was obvious the whole time.' An old man is shaking his head, 'I think I must have dozed off for a bit.' Then I hear, 'That's the trouble with these whodunits, you never really know whodunit.'

I knew whodunit. It was me whodunit.

To my horror, the next day's ship's programme listed the same film to be shown that night as well. I was hoping for a good long break before the next screening. That night, in filed the audience, some probably for a second time trying to work out the plot. Ah well, time to get it over with, face the music and show it all.

Just as the theatre doors were to close, in a blaze of tropical whites and gold braid in came the Italian captain, chief engineer, chief purser, chief steward, ship's doctor and a couple of other senior officers. They took up a standing position at the back of the theatre. My stomach dropped to my socks.

I set the first two reels going and contemplated the third. If I showed it tonight, the ship's officers would all realise I missed out an entire reel the previous night. I wasn't quite sure what the penalty would be for that. Instant dismissal? Court martial? Or maybe a simple keel hauling? I took the coward's way and decided to again not show the third reel. No one would ever know.

To make matters worse, I didn't show the missing reel again on the last night of the cruise. Come the next cruise, the film was still on board for screening, and sure enough, in came all the ship's officers. Later I learned they repeatedly watched all the film screenings to improve their English. That wretched film was on the ship for three more cruises. And I never did show that third reel.

So, to all those moviegoers who must have been puzzling over the movie for decades, I apologise. Forgive me Father, for I have sinned.

Early Life

Despite all this nonsense, I formed a deep attachment to this ship. She started life as MS *Dunnottar Castle* and during her long life she served as a passenger liner, an armed merchant cruiser, a troopship and a cruise ship.

The ship was named after the remains of a ruined medieval fortress built five centuries ago on a cold, bleak and rocky headland on the north-eastern coast of Scotland by a group of knickerless Scots. Just the sort of name you would pick for a glamour ship voyaging from London's Tilbury Dock to the warm climes of South Africa.

In fairness, her owner was Britain's famous Union Castle Line, who named all their numerous ships after various castles in the United Kingdom. I guess to choose this name, they had reached the stage where they were running out of castles.

The ship was to lose something in the glamour stakes with the arrival of the Second World War and the government seized her, along with her sister ship, *Dunvegan Castle*, and made them into armed merchant cruisers with 6in, 3in and anti-aircraft guns and put her on convoy escort duties. In 1942 the British Admiralty went a step further and converted her into a troopship for her to be able to carry soldiers to North Africa and India.

With the long war finished, in 1948, *Dunnottar Castle* was discharged and returned to Union Castle, which promptly had her comprehensively overhauled and returned to her pre-war route. *Dunvegan Castle* was not so lucky. She was sunk in the 1942 Battle of the Atlantic.

In 1958, the Incres Steamship Co. bought *Dunnottar Castle* and spared no expense on turning her into a modern cruise ship. Raking the bow, stripping off the masts, streamlining her funnel and installing new derricks revolution-ised the look of the ship. Down below her cabins were restructured into one class and given a new name along with a shiny brochure extolling the virtues of Caribbean cruising from New York. She was now SS *Victoria*.

I really liked working on her. Maybe because she was comparatively small, she was very warm and intimate. In the crew, everybody knew every-body. Relationships with passengers were good as we also got to know each other. Sometimes too well.

We had on board a very striking, tall, professional dance couple. Most ships carried them, and they used to give dance lessons by day and two or three nights a cruise gave a performance for the evening cabaret. The couple on the *Victoria* were married. Their *pièce de résistance* was the tango, a dance they performed with great heat in an almost violent way.

Every cruise, before they went on, they would work each other up into a rage at the bar, calling each other vile names while they both quickly downed several tequilas. Fascinated by the fiery swirling of the wife's gown, I would crouch down low on the edge of the dance floor to try and capture with my camera some of the passion of the spectacle.

One night, the wife looked at me with round eyes in the crowded bar and hissed loudly, 'That dirty bastard went out in Puerto Rico last night and he got the pox.' There was a sudden silence in the bar. The band started up and on they came. They whirled around the floor and as she swept and dipped in front of me, she brought her face close to mine and snarled in fury, 'He gave it to me!' A few more whirls on the floor and she was thrown down right in front of me. 'It's the third time he's done it!'

Back they came. By now, those in the audience around the dance floor were sitting up straight in their chairs and leaning towards me to hear what would come next. 'Keep away from the dirty bastard.' Round they twirled again. Thrown flat onto her back on the middle of the dance floor, she called out to me, 'He'll have you next!'

Somehow or other, we all remained friends.

Playboy and the Priest

Even the Catholic priest on board was a character. He used to knock on the darkroom door one or two days a week and watch us developing our prints under the glow of a yellow safe light. He would not say much, just stand there smiling, probably praying for our photographer souls.

One day, my colleague, again another young fellow, pulled the centrefold out of a *Playboy* magazine and proudly taped the naked girl to the darkroom wall. I was a bit worried about this, as I was aware of the priest's regular visits, but I didn't want to order my assistant to take it down. Instead, I made a little polka dot paper bikini, carefully cut it out and put it over the usual places but hinged with Sellotape. When my colleague felt the need, he could take a good look and then drop the hinge bikini down for the priest's visit.

The priest came in, spied the poster and studied it intently for a few moments. He then went up to it, lifted the hinges, took a good long look, lowered them back down again and then walked out without saying a word. Two days later, he came back and repeated the procedure and went off with a smirk on his face, still without saying a word. This went on every day for a week. 'Right', I thought, and took the paper bikini right off and left her on the wall in all her glory. When the priest came in, he studied the centrefold for a good long time. We waited for his words of divine wrath. 'Better,' he said, and walked out the door.

One last story about *Victoria*. We had gone back to the Mediterranean for some service work in Italy. I spent quite a bit of time there and had developed a taste for Chianti. As I was walking back to the ship just before we were to leave Genoa for another Caribbean season, I spotted a giant novelty bottle of the stuff in a shop window. It held 15 litres and was a bargain price. Just the thing I needed for another long cruise season on the Caribbean.

I got it back to the ship in its wicker basket and proudly set it on the dressing table in my cabin. By the time the ship reached Gibraltar, I had managed to consume the entire contents of its long neck.

Alas, sailing the smooth waters of the Mediterranean is one thing, but crossing the South Atlantic is a different proposition. First day out, the huge bottle toppled over and smashed onto the fawn-carpeted cabin floor.

When I came back to the cabin, I discovered a tidal wave of the stuff rolling across the carpet from one side of the cabin to the other. A couple of stewards helped me clean it up, but I have been told that fawn carpet stayed pink until the end of the ship's days.

After that I was moved onto another ship and in 1964, she was sold to a subsidiary of the Swedish Clipper Line of Malmö, but Incres Line remained agents for the ship. For the next eleven years *Victoria* cruised the United States to the Caribbean run.

In 1975 Clipper Line sold her to Chandris Line and her name was changed to *The Victoria*. Chandris used her for Caribbean and European cruises until 1993.

In 1993 Louis Cruise Lines bought the ship, renamed her *Princesa Victoria* and used her for three-day cruises from Cyprus.

In 1997 *Princesa Victoria* rescued 487 passengers and 186 crew members from the fiercely burning MV *Romantica*. This was another former ship I had worked on when she was known as MS *Aurelia*.

Victoria was not to last much longer. In 2002, she was the longest-serving passenger ship of her size in the world. The time had come to retire her. She sat at the dock for a while to see if another suitor could be found. This was without success and in 2004 *Victoria* arrived in India for scrapping.

26

RMS *Windsor Castle*
(Later SS *Margarita L*)

The cruise ship *Margarita L* (RMS *Windsor Castle*), laid up in Eleusis Bay in 2002.
(Peter J. Fitzpatrick, CCA SA 4.0, via WikimediaCommons)

Born	1960
Died	2005
GRT	37,640
Length	784ft
Beam	94ft
Passengers	782
Crew	475
Line	Union Castle

On Time, Every Time

In the first half of the last century, British passenger shipping was dominated by four companies with routes to the four corners of the world. They serviced the trade routes to the former British colonies, transporting settlers, tourists, businesspeople and the honoured right to carry the British Royal Mail. Cunard operated to the USA, Shaw Savill travelled to Australia and New Zealand, as did P&O, which also serviced India and the East, while Union Castle Line took passengers to South Africa, mostly via Madeira.

Union Castle ships were named after famous British castles and were known for their livery of a lavender hull and a red funnel with a black band at the top, and for departing to such a strict schedule that people in Southampton could set their clocks by them.

For years, every Thursday, dead on the dot of 4 p.m., one liner would leave Southampton for Cape Town, while at the same time, another would depart from Cape Town for Southampton. As the ships got faster and reduced the transit time from thirteen days to eleven days, the Southampton departure time was changed to Fridays at 1 p.m.

The pride and last flagship of the Union Castle fleet was *Windsor Castle*. She was the queen bee, larger, more modern, more beautiful and more luxurious than the rest. She was built on Merseyside and, although not particularly big by today's standards, at the time she was the largest liner ever built in England.

It was Scotland that built Cunard's bigger Queens – a part of Britain to be sure, but not England. For our American cousins, I must mention that a failure to recognise this distinction is at your peril. Nevertheless, she was launched by the popular Queen Mother, not with a bottle of London gin, but with a bottle of South African bubbly.

After successful sea trials and before her maiden voyage in August 1960, she made a brief delivery sailing with Union Castle office staff acting as passengers. An excellent idea which should be adopted by all new ships. The cost to the company to do this would be huge. However, it would also benefit the company enormously. Not only is it good staff relations, but it also gave the stewards and galley crew a chance for a practise run with passengers who were not paying customers.

She proved a very comfortable and reliable ship and quickly became known to passengers and crew as the *Windsor*. Her first-class furnishings were traditional, even conservative, while tourist class was equipped in a more modern style. She had all the facilities: two outdoor swimming pools, a spa, a theatre-cum-cinema and a hospital.

The carrying of cargo was also an important function of the ship. Apart from carrying the Royal Mail, she had a large amount of dry and refrigerated cargo space, cargo wine tanks and a secure room for the storage of bullion. She even had a garage for the transport of cars.

Fire? Have a Cup of Tea

In 1967 and late one evening while berthed in Durban, an electrical fire broke out on Shaw Saville's *Northern Star*. As a precautionary measure all her passengers were evacuated onto the dockside. There was nowhere for them to go.

Taking pity on them was the captain of *Windsor Castle*, which was overnighting on the same length of dock and moored immediately behind her. He invited the stranded passengers to take tea, coffee and sandwiches in the *Windsor*'s saloon. At 4 a.m., the fire on the *Northern Star* had been safely extinguished and the passengers were able to return to their ship, but they were extremely grateful for the courtesy shown by the crew of *Windsor Castle*.

The Eerie Tale of the Dirty Porthole

The older crew members of a liner seem to love spinning yarns of ghosts and mysterious things that go bump in the night to their newbies. A ship at sea is the ideal setting for spinning such yarns, with the hull plates creaking and groaning, the clanking of the steel chain through the hawser and the swaying motion of the ocean.

On *Windsor*, they loved to relate the story of the dirty porthole. When the ship was docked in Durban, the crew walking along the dock saw that the glass of one of the portholes was very dirty. It looked as though it had never been cleaned.

With the ship under way, the crew looked at all the cabins from the inside and could not find it. All the portholes were cleaned perfectly. Yet at the next stop, walking along the dock they found the dirty porthole was still there. Taking careful note of its position on the ship, the crew went in search of the porthole, but again could not find it.

It was a calm day at sea so, frustrated, they lowered a sailor over the side in a bosun's chair to check for it again. He found it and got up close and peered in. He reported he could see the cabin inside but could not see a door opening into the cabin.

The crew decided to make a full-scale search of the decks above and below the porthole, tapping on all the bulkheads and partitions. In the crew's quarters, they found a wall that sounded hollow. An officer ordered the wall to be broken down. Once through, they discovered the cabin the sailor saw, but it didn't have a porthole.

The crew realised the cabin must have been walled in while *Windsor* was being built, but that still didn't explain the missing porthole. They boarded up the cabin again and posted a guard. They then sent the sailor over the side again to check for the porthole. It was still there, but on looking through it, the sailor could not see any sign of the broken wall that had just been boarded up.

So how does the story end? Well, *Windsor*'s captain ordered the rumours to be shut down, but new crew members going ashore kept looking for the dirty porthole.

I sometimes wonder if it was a ruse to make sure the glass in all the portholes was always kept shiny, or possibly it was a story made up as they had no access to Netflix in those days.

The Tortoise and the Hare

In 1967, Union Castle promoted *Windsor* as the fastest way to get from Southampton to Cape Town after air. The Ford Motor Company chose to dispute this and challenged *Windsor Castle* to a race on the return leg to Southampton. Sticking to their guns, Union Castle accepted the challenge.

Ford pitted its Liverpool, Merseyside-built Corsair 2000E against the Merseyside-built *Windsor Castle*. The ship and the car left simultaneously from the dock at Cape Town, with the *Windsor Castle* facing a 7,000-mile voyage and the Corsair a 9,700-mile road journey offering numerous potential pitfalls.

The Corsair hit a water-filled pothole 6ft deep, faced difficulty getting petrol, harassment by armed Congolese soldiers, twenty-four tyre changes and thirty-seven puncture repairs. Nearing Southampton, the car was pulled over by the police for having a dirty number plate.

Meanwhile, *Windsor Castle* sailed serenely on. But the Corsair arrived the evening before *Windsor* docked. However, when penalties were considered, it was declared a draw. It was a good publicity stunt for both companies.

A Million to One Chance

Early one morning in 1976, when the ship was between Las Palmas and Cape Town, a 64-year-old British lady managed to accidentally fall over the side into the ocean. Her fall was unseen. She may have been at the stern gazing down at the prop wash. It can have a hypnotic effect that draws you in. Never gaze at it alone, particularly at night.

An hour later, the husband reported his wife as missing. A search was made without success and the captain decided he must turn back and attempt the almost impossible task of finding her.

Reversing the bearing in those day wasn't always easy because of winds and currents, but the captain did get some clues from rubbish floating in the sea tossed overboard during their previous passage. Ships jettisoning rubbish into the ocean was common practice in those days, but it is certainly no longer allowed.

Incredibly, an hour later they found her. She had survived two hours in shark-infested water, mainly because it was warm and presumably because the sharks had already had their breakfast. The liner stopped and lowered a lifeboat to retrieve her. The captain described it as 'a million to one chance'.

A Second Life

A combined assault of high oil prices, airline competition and the widespread political upheavals in South Africa, making it a much less attractive destination for new settlers, led to a loss of passenger traffic and *Windsor Castle* had to be sold. On 12 August 1977, she sailed from Southampton for her 124th and final sailing for Union Castle. The city gave her a huge send-off and an RAF fly-past.

She was bought by the Greek oil and shipping magnate Yiannis Latsis. In October, sporting the Latsis Line colours on her funnel and the name *Margarita L* on her stern, she departed Southampton for the last time and was on her way to Greece.

When *Margarita L*, named after one of Latsis' daughters, arrived at Piraeus, the famous lavender hull was painted white, and she was converted into an office, luxury accommodation and leisure centre for Latsis' own company and berthed at Rabigh and Jeddah in Saudi Arabia.

At Jeddah she was docked in a complex with swimming pools, sports facilities and a car park. A helipad was added to the ship just aft of the former first-class pool area.

In 1990 she was towed to Eleusis, Greece, to be laid up. Yiannis Latsis would often stay on board. He took great pride in the ship, keeping her well maintained and furnished with all the original Union Castle fittings.

After he died, his son had little interest in the ship, and she fell into appalling neglect. In England, a move was made to bring her home to serve as a hotel ship, but the idea did not gain traction.

In December 2004 she was sold for scrap and renamed *Rita* for her last journey to the graveyard. She set off under her own steam, but her heart finally gave out and her engines broke down. A tug had to be sent to tow her to her final destination. The tug also broke down, but it was repaired and finished the tow to the breakers on an Indian beach.

She was the last of Union Castle's ships to go. As *Windsor Castle*, she made 124 round-trip voyages, carried 270,000 passengers and travelled more than 1.6 million nautical miles. On the day of this great British liner's 45th anniversary maiden voyage from Southampton, the breakers began their work of total destruction.

27

SS *France*

(Later SS *Norway* and SS *Blue Lady*)

SS *France*.

Born	1962
Died	2006
GRT	66,343
Length	1,035ft
Beam	34ft
Passengers	1,944
Crew	1,253
Line	French Line, or Compagnie Générale Transatlantique

Oo-La-La on the Atlantic

January 1962: I am 19, standing with a small group of friends at the end of Southampton Water's Hythe Pier. As far as the eye can see, the foreshore is thronged with people. Offshore, there is a large flotilla of small boats and ten pleasure steamers milling about. Crowding their decks are spectators in their hundreds. They have forked out £5 to get a closer look at the spectacle about to unfold.

From the distance we hear a ship's whistle booming out. Another ship calls back. Now there are a dozen or more ships, all blasting away. Why do they call them whistles when their booming shakes through to the soul? Their noise is building to a crescendo of deafening booming, and now a sudden roar from the crowd tries to outdo them.

We can see the tops of her remarkable two funnels with their futuristic space-age wings. They are moving slowly, inch by inch, as she is tugged clear of the dock.

Around a bend in the river, she finally comes into full view. This is SS *France*, the new pride and joy of a country eager to regain its mark on transatlantic travel.

She is now broadside to our pier. We take in the full sweep of her decks, the stylish superstructure and those amazing funnels. She is lean and long. Incredibly long. In fact, she is now the longest liner in the world.

I feel a pang: rueful regret, jealousy, begrudging admiration? I don't know how to describe it. I was working on a humble Greek cruise ship and yet to work on *Queen Mary* as the cabin-class entertainment officer, but it was always my ambition to sail with Cunard.

With all the Anglo-French rivalry, it almost seemed disloyal to be giving such an enthusiastic reception to a French ship. She was out to rival our beloved but aging *Queen Mary* and *Queen Elizabeth*. Cunard already had to cope with the introduction of SS *United States*, which although smaller, was newer and faster on the Atlantic crossings. And now this. I content myself with the thought that although the two Queens are not as long, they are at least bigger.

Making matters even less palatable was the bombastic boasting of French President Charles de Gaulle. His wife, Yvonne, did the honours of the actual launching, but de Gaulle gave a patriotic speech boasting France would regain the mantle once worn by *Normandie*, able to compete with Cunard's Queens, and that the Atlantic speed record was within reach.

He called enthusiastically, '*Vive le France, Vive la France!*' No, he wasn't getting his French male and female genders mixed up. Along with other peculiarities of the French, such as eating snails and frogs legs, they have the odd habit of calling ships 'he'. So in the case of *France*, the use of 'le' is justified.

He also called to the crowd at the launching ceremony, 'I have given you a new *Normandie!*' And he had indeed. Maybe not as grand, but certainly, in her way, just as beautiful.

De Gaulle was a staunch defender of her design. When it was pointed out to him the ship was too long to fit though the Suez Canal, he said, '*Non*, the canal is too short to fit *Le France.*' He must have momentarily forgotten that the canal was also designed by a Frenchman.

He had every right to be proud as he was one of the main proponents for her to be built. French Line, or to give its proper name, Compagnie Générale Transatlantique, was planning on building two smaller ships for its transatlantic fleet. But de Gaulle championed the idea it was better for national pride to build one grand liner as an ocean-going showcase for France.

The shipping company would not agree to the expense and called for public funding for such a venture. This caused a national debate and the controversy would last three and a half years before the deal between the government and the company was struck.

Her construction introduced a new way of shipbuilding. Aluminium was used in the superstructure, welding replaced riveting in many areas and modules of the ship were built off site and then installed in the ship. The development of improved engine power also allowed the number of boilers to be reduced to six. She was never the fastest, that honour belonged to SS *United States*, but her looks, standards of service, style and gourmet food made her the envy of the shipping world.

The rich and famous booked passage on her: Salvador Dalí, Cary Grant, Audrey Hepburn, Andy Warhol, Tennessee Williams, the Beatles and that most famous lady of all, the *Mona Lisa*. *France* was entrusted with the task of transporting the famous painting to the United States for exhibition.

For the first-class area of the ship, France used its very best designers to create the most stunning interiors at sea. Nowhere was this more evident than in the public rooms.

The dining room was a blaze of gold-anodised aluminium under a back-painted dome, filled with recessed spotlights and surrounded by a circular band of fluorescent lit panels. It was the perfect setting for what was to become known as the 'best French restaurant in the world'.

The French carried their passion for excellence to extremes and went so far as to even offer the pets accompanying their owners a deluxe special menu of their own. The dog kennels took a leaf out of Cunard's book of offering British dogs a lamp post and US dogs a fire hydrant; the French did the same, only replacing the lamp post with a Parisian milestone.

Insane Unions

She sailed for French Line for thirteen years, but like the other great ocean liners, she had to face the decline in the transatlantic trade caused by the increasing popularity of air travel. Rising fuel costs and a growing reluctance of the French Government to help with her running costs was making for financial difficulties.

In the winter season, she followed the trend of abandoning the crossings and turned to cruising as a one-class ship. However, although she came to the party late for Atlantic crossings, she was ill-designed as a cruise ship. She was short on deck space and had no outside pools. Despite these flaws, she was popular at the beginning, but it was not to last.

When the price of crude oil in 1973 went from $3 to $12 per barrel, keeping *France* operating was costing the French Government an additional $10 million a year. They decided to switch allegiance and put their money instead into the enemy: the Concorde supersonic airliner.

It was announced in 1974 that *France* would be withdrawn. Now the French seamen's union proved itself as equally insane as the British version in 1966. Proving no lessons had been learned, they went on strike, demanding an extra 35 per cent pay rise for themselves and that *France* should continue. It was an exercise in making an unprofitable ship more unprofitable.

When the ship reached Le Havre, the union moored her across the harbour entrance, preventing any ship from entering or leaving the port. The 1,200 passengers on board had to be ferried ashore, but the crew stayed on board in a Mexican standoff.

You can imagine how that played out. After a little over a month of sitting there, the strikers gave up this futile exercise and the ship was berthed in Le Havre harbour. It became known as the pier of the forgotten.

And forgotten she was, as the former pride of France, with all furnishings and fittings intact, sat neglected for four years. There was talk of potential suitors: an Arab millionaire wanting to purchase her as an art museum, another planning to operate her as a casino in the United States. The Russians thought she would make a good floating hotel in the Black Sea, while the Chinese wanted to use her as a floating exhibition centre.

From Pride of France to Pride of Norway

The successful bid in 1979 was from Norwegian Caribbean Line (NCL), a company with deep pockets prepared to fork out $18 million for the ship and then spend another $80 million to convert her into the world's biggest cruise ship. So the former national pride of France was to become SS *Norway*, the national pride of Norway. And just to make sure there was no mistake about it, the classic black hull with red boot-topping, white superstructure and red funnels were repainted a shameful shade of blue. I suspect I'm guilty of being a bit of a traditionalist.

The clean look of the superstructure also suffered as vast areas of deck were opened up. This included a large lido deck and outdoor pool necessary for sunbathing cruise passengers.

Most importantly, the Norwegians set about dealing with her fuel-guzzling engines. Now able to proceed in cruising mode, the forward engine room was dismantled and two of her propellers were removed. To save the expensive use of tugs when docking, they also fitted bow and stern thrusters so she could dock unaided.

She was to be based in Miami for Caribbean cruising. As she set off in her new livery, the city of Southampton gave her a second rousing send-off.

SS *Norway* enjoyed great success as a cruise ship, prompting other shipping companies to build increasingly bigger and better cruise ships to compete. Even NCL began introducing newer ships of their own to put SS *Norway* in the shade.

In 2003, while docked in Miami, a boiler explosion caused superheated steam to pour into the boiler room and the crew cabins above. The accident killed eight members of her crew and injured seventeen others.

Once towed back to a Bremerhaven shipyard, a detailed examination revealed she was beyond economic repair. In March 2004, NCL declared she would never sail again as SS *Norway*. Ownership was transferred to NCL's parent company, who opted to rename her *Blue Lady*.

However, large amounts of asbestos, mostly discovered in the engine rooms, meant she was initially not allowed to leave Germany due to the Basel Convention protecting health at sea. However, once it was explained she was to be towed to Asia for repairs and made suitable for cruising from Australia, she was given the green light to proceed.

She remained anchored off the Indian coast while Greenpeace, and other environmental organisations, protested to the Indian government over the health risk she posed. In India, an inspection by experts was ordered and the report came back saying she was safe to be scrapped. The accuracy of the report was roundly criticised, but in 2008, they began stripping this once pride of France.

A part of her was returned to France. A small section of the bow was auctioned off, purchased and mounted on public display at the Paris Yacht Marina. In May 2017, the city of Le Havre bought it for €171,600 and relocated it to their city's cruise terminal. This time it is not blocking the entrance to the port but remains an ignominious pointed end for a once proud ship.

28

MV *Stella Polaris*

MV *Stella Polaris*.

Born	1926
Died	2006
GRT	5,209
Length	416ft
Beam	51ft
Cruise speed	15 knots
Passengers	150–214
Crew	100–130
Line	Clipper Line

The Beauty of Being Small

By 1965 I had become familiar with many of the world's seaports as my London-based company, specialising in ship's photography, sent me from ship to ship as a relieving on-board photo unit manager. I had joined a variety of ships in such places as New York, Boston, Genoa and Southampton, but never had I been sent to Harwich. This was then a very small port on the Essex coast in the south-east of England and although I knew the town had a ferry to Holland, I could not imagine a passenger ship ever fitting into such a small haven.

My bosses had sent me here with only two days' notice to join her as a last-minute replacement. They had no chance to give me a proper briefing and all I knew was my new ship was called *Stella Polaris*, was formerly Norwegian but now Swedish owned and she did world cruising as well as trips to the North Cape and the Mediterranean.

Getting off the train from London in Harwich, there was not a glimpse of any passenger ship to be seen. No funnels broke the skyline and there was none of the usual boarding hustle and bustle at the railway station.

However, an obliging taxi driver found her and deposited me on a small dock at the foot of her gangway. I gaped. Before me was something like an early steamer with a long nose and a bowsprit. This was more private yacht than any suggestion of a passenger ship.

In previous years I had worked on ships from 38,000 tons to as small as 15,000 tons, but now London must be joking. To put it in proportion, the *Stella* was a tad over 5,000 tons, which made her a fortieth of the size of today's cruise ships. I checked my boarding paperwork again and the name on the vessel's stern. They matched, so up the gangway I marched to find not a single soul insight.

I wandered around freely. I decided to start at the top and checked in at the bridge. There was no one there. No officer of the watch, no master of arms. Surprising. But even more surprising was the bridge itself, a very simple affair with lots of polished brass. Later I was to discover that originally the bridge had been completely open to the air.

In the 1930s, from the Arctic and across the Equator she would go with the bridge offering little protection for the poor bridge officers. I imagined mahogany-faced sailors with icy beards gripping binoculars with thickly gloved hands and swaddled in layers of cable-knit, polo-neck jerseys, topped off with long duffle coats. They must have been a tough lot.

The small boat deck hosted four lifeboats and there was a motorised tender on each side. Spartan, but I guessed and prayed that was all that was needed.

Down the companionway and onto a small promenade deck, I found the music salon, a veranda café and a smoking room. Oh my! Very classy. Everything exuded luxury.

On C deck I found a magnificent dining room with rich carpeting and fine furniture set for between 100 and 150 guests. On the ceiling was a mass of coloured lamps arranged to form a star. Very impressive. Definitely a place for millionaires. I guess it was more the private luxury yacht you have when you don't already have one of your own.

Six to a Cabin

Coming back up the companionways, I ran into a tall Swedish man in a steward's black uniform sporting two silver stripes on his sleeve. He welcomed me aboard and explained nearly all the crew were ashore as the passengers were not due to embark for another three hours. He took me along to see the chief steward in his cabin. It appeared that, outside navigation and mechanical duties, he was the man that ran the ship.

His stewards were mostly blond male Scandinavian types who lived crammed cheek by jowl in the confines of the fo'c'sle. As I was a 'foreigner' representing a concession holder, he said I could have a passenger cabin and drink socially at the bar, but I must remember his word was law. The offer of a passenger cabin was a relief as I had noted the crew accommodation mainly consisted of four or six to a cabin.

Can you imagine six young blokes living together in the confines of a small space? Probably best not. However, this was quite common on ships in those days, but so far, a nightmarish hell I had the good fortune to avoid. So, it was to be a passenger cabin for me. This was a particular bonus as these passenger cabins were very classy affairs furnished in fine woods. Jackpot.

He asked what other ships I had worked on and I reeled off six well-known liners. He sniffed. His passengers, he insisted were a very elite and a special group and I was not under any circumstances to take a photograph of any passenger unless they specifically requested it.

I gulped. How on earth was I going to make money for my company under such circumstances? I didn't. But I had a wonderful trip up to the

North Cape and the Land of the Midnight Sun. Plus I went to some of the best crew parties of my life.

I fear that at such revelries I might have been fed some dubious stories. I was told the ship was ordered to be built by the exiled Kaiser Wilhelm II. However, although the Kaiser had a penchant for the occasional personal yacht and didn't die until 1941, I cannot find any historical record of *Stella* having been originally commissioned by him.

These doubts are fuelled by the fact that at this merry party I was told that during the Second World War *Stella* was at one time sunk across a fjord in Norway to prevent the Germans entering. However, the invasion succeeded, and the Germans raised *Stella* and converted her into a floating brothel for the recreational use of U-boat submariners.

Quite a story. And, as a matter of fact, I do believe the last part is true. History does indeed record the captured *Stella Polaris* was used as a 'rest and recreation' boat for German U-boat crews. And we can all imagine what that entailed. After all, US Navy folklore claims that a liberty boat is seven sailors with seven oars. However, I cannot find any record of *Stella* ever being sunk as a blockade ship. But it was a wonderful party.

Stella Polaris was commissioned by a Norwegian company called Bergen, a forerunner of Royal Viking Lines, and they claimed she was the first designed and purpose-built cruise ship. If she was not the actual first, she certainly was among the very first.

Work was started in Sweden by Götaverken in Gothenburg in 1925 and she was launched with great fanfare and media acclaim in September 1926 by Miss Lehmkuhl, the daughter of Bergen Steamships' director.

An early passenger was the famous English writer Evelyn Waugh, who made his Mediterranean cruise the subject of his first travel book: *Labels*. Wrote Waugh: 'She was certainly a very pretty ship, standing rather high in the water, with the tail-pointed prow of a sailing yacht, white all over except for her single yellow funnel, and almost ostentatiously clean ...'

Stella's career nearly came to an early end in 1937 when she was in a collision with another vessel carrying a cargo of dynamite and ammunition. Fortunately for *Stella*, the munitions vessel, *Nobel*, sunk, taking her dangerous cargo with her. *Stella*'s bow was damaged, and her previously famous long bow sprit was dramatically shortened. For manoeuvrability the captains must have decided this was a great improvement as it was never returned to its former length.

Although the Great Depression had not seemed to impact her cruise bookings for the Mediterranean, North Cape and around-the-world cruises, the Second World War did. Norway tried for a neutral role, but Hitler was looking for some ice-free ports for his navy to control the Atlantic approaches to Britain. So, he invaded Norway. The excuse used was that Germany wanted to protect Norway from the British and the French.

The outbreak of war put an immediate end to cruises and *Stella* was laid up in Oslo until the German troops landed in Norway. In an attempt to conceal her from the enemy, she was immediately moved into the wilds of Osterfjorden, but seven months later she was found and seized by German forces. For the next three years she flew the German flag and provided her comforts to U-boat crews.

At the end of the war, she came under the management of the Ministry of War Transport and was used to transport Russian prisoners of war to Murmansk. She also helped repatriate many of the troops.

When, in 1945, she was finally handed back to Bergen Line, she had been thoroughly and utterly trashed. All the fine furnishings had been ripped apart and the artworks had gone. The departing Germans thought that if they couldn't have her, nor should anyone else. Oddly enough, out of respect, or the fact that they were out of sight, the engines were still in good condition.

Bergen returned the ship to the builder's yard for complete repair, restoration and the installation of a new ventilation system. This was completed in eight months, but at a cost that was more than the original build. To meet new safety regulations, the number of cabins was reduced to a capacity for 189 passengers. This created the space for a new dance salon.

With a very varied cruise itinerary, *Stella* stayed with Bergen until the company accepted an offer from the Swedish Clipper Line. The offer did not include the numerous artworks on board, so these were taken off and the ship sent for another makeover, which apart from new carpeting and artworks, included the installation of air conditioning.

Back in service at the end of 1951, she now sailed under the Swedish flag, but resumed a similar cruise itinerary, although without the world cruise offer. But her reputation as being one of the finest and most luxurious afloat continued to build.

She did have her adventures. While cruising the fjords, a massive rock fall from the sheer cliffs nearly hit and sank *Stella*. On another cruise one young lady passenger with a broken heart committed suicide by jumping into the cold waters off the south coast of Sweden. Apparently, her parents had decreed she was not to marry her Australian soldier sweetheart.

On-board food storage was limited, so orders were cabled ahead of the ship's arrival. In Calais, there was a major communication break-down and an order for 400 flowers to decorate the ship resulted in the delivery of a ton of cauliflowers – not quite the décor the chief steward had in mind.

She was also the victim of a robbery. Her priceless art collections had already been through trials and tribulations both during the war and in the change of ownership, but in one of her refits in 1968, while in her home port of Malmo, thieves managed to raid the new artwork.

In spite of this, Clipper Line maintained *Stella Polaris* in top order throughout her life, but while she had plenty of bookings, the aging ship was having trouble meeting the new maritime safety laws. This led to most refits having to reduce the number of passengers carried and by 1954 she was only licensed for 155.

But worse was to come in 1968 when, to meet the latest regulations, new refrigeration and storage facilities on board had to be built to meet hygiene standards, reducing the number of passenger cabins to just seventy. Gradually, but surely, *Stella* was being squeezed out of existence.

She was still a fine ship and a fine place to be but the cold fact was that it was no longer financially wise to keep this marvellous, unique ship in ser-vice. Forgive old-fashioned me, but I doubt the word 'unique' has crossed my keyboard before as I respect it's true meaning of one and only and shud-der at the mere thought of modifiers such as 'almost', 'most' and 'totally'. *Stella Polaris* is indeed fully deserving of the use of the word unique. Nevertheless, she was put up for sale.

She was sold in 1969 to be a floating hotel in Japan. Her thirty pieces of silver amounted to $850,000. In October that year she left Lisbon flying the Japanese flag.

On arrival, the two propellers were removed. This last act of violation was to enable lower taxes by classifying her as a building and not a ship. But the name *Stella Polaris* was still on her bows.

After the novelty waned, business suffered, and the hotel operation was shut down. But tourist visitors and the restaurant remained open, offering a Scandinavian-style smorgasbord. They were all the rage those days.

After more than thirty years in Japan, there was a movement gathering in Sweden to bring her back. If she was to be a floating restaurant and hotel, why couldn't she do this in Stockholm? The deal was done and the old lady was to be patched up to make the trip home to the land of her birth.

However, a Chinese company was engaged to prepare her for her voyage back across the world. But while they had her under tow to Shanghai for the preparation work, she gave up the ghost. On 2 September 2006, she sank in 70m of water just south of Nagoya.

So no, she wasn't sunk as a blockade ship in the Second World War. This classic ship was sunk by the Chinese in 2006.

29

Costa Concordia

Costa Concordia. (Cezary Piwowarski, CCA SA 4.0, via Wikimedia Commons)

Born	2005
Died	2012
GRT	114,137
Length	952ft
Beam	116ft
Passengers	3,780
Crew	1,100
Line	Costa Crociere Line
Sister ships	*Costa Serena, Pacifica, Favolosa* and *Fascinosa*

A Captain's Shame

It started to go wrong on the day of the launch. At the dock, a VIP viewing stand was erected and a large, enthusiastic audience assembled around the bow of the biggest cruise ship Italy had ever built.

The air was filled with cheers as fashion model Eva Herzigová swung down the traditional bottle of champagne. But on the first attempt the bottle did not break. Groans mixed with a few boos escaped the horrified crowd. A second successful attempt was greeted with a restrained smattering of polite applause. For sailors and ship owners, for the christening bottle not to break is akin to the kiss of death.

And so it proved to be. First came the 2008 incident in Palermo, when strong winds pushed the ship into a dock, causing severe damage to her miss-anointed bow. Fortunately, other than to the ship herself, there were no injuries and in a month the repairs were done. But her good looks were tarnished by the look of the big dents still visible in her hull.

She carried these blemishes until 2011, when a major refurbishment saw the scars finally erased. But not for long. The very next year, she fatally struck coastal rocks and sank with the loss of thirty-two lives.

In those pre-Brexit days, the name *Concordia* was chosen to express continuing harmony, unity and peace between European nations. Accordingly, her thirteen passenger decks were named after member countries: Holland, Germany, France, Italy, Great Britain and so on. Choosing the pecking order must have been a nightmare, but for once, Poland ended up on top.

Appealing to a wide range of nationalities, *Costa Concordia* proved a popular cruise ship. Of her 1,500 cabins, 505 had private balconies and there were fifty-eight suites for the well-heeled.

The public facilities were also good. The two-level fitness centre was one of the largest at sea and featured a spa, gym, thalassotherapy pool, sauna, Turkish bath and a solarium. If anyone is unsure of exactly what a thalassotherapy pool is, I understand it to mean it has saltwater and sea air: a couple of things one would have thought not to be totally unexpected on a cruise ship. Moving on, two of the four pools had retractable roofs, plus there were five jacuzzies and even a poolside movie theatre.

The less athletic were also well catered for with five restaurants, thirteen bars, one designated as a cigar and cognac bar (remember those?), a three-level theatre, a casino and a super whizz-bang disco.

Children could be sent off to a fun play area equipped with video games and a basketball court. Kids would be well entertained while parents enjoyed a few hours of respite.

With such facilities, she should have had a long and successful career, but in calm waters, a dreadful navigational error ended her seagoing days. With all the modern navigational aids and electronic positioning, how on earth could a modern ship make such a woeful mistake? After sailing from the Rome port of Civitavecchia, she was on the first leg of a seven-day Mediterranean cruise under the command of Captain Francesco Schettino. She was not to get far.

Lack of a $5 Glass Cutter

The decision is made to deviate from her plotted course to sail close to the island of Isola del Giglio, a few miles off Italy's Tuscany coast.

On the bridge is the Italian captain, dark and handsome. So is a pretty Moldovan dancer, who was on board as a non-paying passenger. There are reports that before the incident, the two had been seen kissing. She later testified she was in a relationship with the captain. Other guests were also reported to be on the bridge.

Whatever the captain's reasons for changing the plotted course, the route they are now sailing has not been computer programmed for this spur-of-the-moment course variation. The alarms for the ship's navigation systems are switched off. The captain is navigating through the night by sight, confident he knows these waters and their seabeds well.

In the darkness, his ship is just 300m from the shore, which is not much more than the length of his vessel. When you are driving a ship of 114,000 plus gross registered tons late at night, that's damn close.

Navigating by sight he may be, but the captain discovers he has not got his reading glasses and therefore cannot read the radar signal. This gives a clear indication of the distance off from the shore. Instead, he is relying on reports from his first officer.

Breaking water on a reef ahead catches the captain's eye and the wheel is spun seawards. But it is too little too late as the turn swings the ship's port side into the reef and it hits a rock. It tears a 160ft-long hole below the waterline wide open to the sea.

In a dining room they hear a loud bang and a jolt. Ironically, allegedly playing over the speakers is Celine Dion's *My Heart Will Go On*, the theme from the movie *Titanic*.

In a move to calm the instant panic, a crew member makes an announcement over the Tannoy system that it is just an electrical failure. Everything is OK and under control.

But it isn't. The ship is shaking, dishes are crashing to the floor and passengers are fleeing up the stairs.

The *Concordia* is taking on water and takes a sudden steep list to port. The engine rooms start to flood and power is lost. The ship begins to drift and lists in the opposite direction, making it extremely difficult to launch the lifeboats. The order to abandon ship was not given until an hour after the ship hit the rocks.

Passenger video shows passengers struggling into their life jackets while being told everything is under control and to go back to their cabins. Against all regulations, a lifeboat drill has not been given to the 600 new passengers joining in Civitavecchia. It's too late now. Almost half of *Concordia* remains above water, but it is in imminent danger of sinking completely into a trough 230ft deep.

Local motorboats come to rescue those in the water while others elect to swim for the shore. Five helicopters fly a continuous operation, airlifting passengers off the ship and carrying them to safety.

Jumping overboard with a life jacket is dangerous if you don't hold it down firmly when you jump. Hitting the water, the jacket may rise up and break your neck. Seven were injured in their attempt and three were drowned. The local island fire chief later said his men plucked 100 people from the water and saved around sixty others trapped in the listing cruise ship.

Thirty minutes before midnight, there are still 300 passengers on the half-sunken ship, but the captain is gone. He will claim he accidentally fell into a lifeboat. In a radio call, an irate coastguard repeatedly orders Captain Schettino to return and take charge of the ongoing evacuation. In utter exasperation, he allegedly finally roars a phrase in Italian that can be mostly translated as, 'Get on board, for f★★★'s sake!'*

* Lizzy Davies, 'Anger as Costa Concordia "hero" transferred to coastguard admin duties', *The Guardian*, 25 September 2014 (www.theguardian.com/world/2014/sep/25/costa-concordia-hero-coastguard-gregorio-de-falco-italy).

Costa Concordia. (Horacio Arevalo, CC A SA 3.0 via WikmiediaCommons)

But Schettino never returned. The phrase, however, quickly found fame and was notoriously quoted on the internet and printed on thousands of t-shirts.

Schettino was not the first captain to opt for an early departure from an emergency scene. In 1991, another ship I once sailed on, Epirotiki's *Oceanos*, hit severe weather off South Africa. There was an explosion heard in the engine room and water flooded in. First away were many crew members, including Captain Yiannis Avranas. Avranas, who thought he could better direct rescue operations from a helicopter, was quoted as saying, 'When I give the order abandon ship, it doesn't matter what time I leave. Abandonment is for everybody. If some people want to stay, they can stay.'*

The hero in that disaster turned out to be Moss Hills, a guitarist and singer on the entertainment staff. Moss went to the abandoned bridge to send out the first Mayday calls and with his wife and other members of the cruise staff, organised the evacuation. Moss was the last to leave.

You might think that after that he would have decided to chuck a career at sea, but it was again Moss who proved to be a hero in the sinking of *Achille Lauro*, a story in Chapter 21.

---

* You can read more about maritime law here: www.dw.com/en/
when-is-a-captain-allowed-to-abandon-ship/a-15674434

International maritime law requires all passengers to be evacuated within thirty minutes of the order to abandon ship. Reports say it took *Costa Concordia* more than six hours to evacuate 3,206 passengers and 1,023 crew.

Although the incident happened so close to the shore, sixty-three people were injured and thirty-three perished. This was made up of twenty-seven passengers, five crew and a member of the salvage team.

The inevitable official criminal investigation found Schettino guilty of manslaughter, causing a shipwreck and of abandoning his passengers, and he was sentenced to sixteen years in prison.

Under the eyes of the world's television cameras, the protracted attempts to avoid an environmental oil disaster and right the ship ready for towing were viewed by millions. Less noticeable was the amount of looting going on. Jewellery, furniture and artwork, up to and including the ship's bell, were stolen by thieves gaining access via the entrances cut through the hull by the search and rescue teams.

The salvage operation was to take three years before the ship could finally be towed away to Genoa for scrapping. Adding up victims' compensation awards, salvage operations, refloating, towing and scrapping, the total cost is estimated at $2 billion – more than three times the original build cost of $612 million. However, more optimistic accountants claimed the world's biggest marine salvage public works project succeeded in injecting more than $1 billion into the Italian economy.

Whichever, but when launching ships, it is vital to ensure the champagne bottle bursts on the first go. The trick is to first scour carefully through half the thickness of the bottle with a $5 glass cutter.

30

MS *Pacific Princess*
(Formerly MS *Sea Venture* and later MS *Pacific*)

MS *Pacific Princess*, aka 'The Love Boat', off the US west coast in 1987. (Dashers at English Wikipedia)

Born	1971
Died	2013
GRT	20,636
Length	553ft
Beam	81ft
Passengers	717
Crew	350
Line	Princess Cruises

Pioneer of Popular Cruising

Launched as *Sea Venture*, this is the ship that did so much to change the face of cruising. She began life operating for Flagship Cruises on the run from the United States to Bermuda, but it was not until she was sold to Princess Cruises that she found television fame as *The Love Boat*.

In 1975, television producer Aaron Spelling approached Princess Cruises about filming a new television show at sea. At first, the company officials did not exactly leap around with joy at the thought of having a television film company trailing cables all over one of their beautiful cruise ships.

When it was learned that Spelling said he merely wanted to 'shoot a pilot', this caused momentary alarm. Company officials valued their pilots and didn't fancy the idea of one of them being shot.

Once everything was explained and seeing the publicity that could flow, Spelling was allowed to shoot his television pilot on board *Sun Princess*. The networks not only loved it, but they wanted a complete series.

Having crossed this hurdle, it was decided to use the newly acquired and larger *Pacific Princess* for the filming. The first episode went to air in 1977 and proved an instant ratings success. It became one of the world's most watched television shows.

The nine-season series went on and on, and then on and on. Just when you thought it was finally finished, the repeats started.

Beginning the Cruising Boom

On board the real *Pacific Princess*, business boomed, and the frequently televised berths could not be filled fast enough. The television series made the ship the most talked about since *Titanic*.

The great thing about the filming of all those high jinks was that it totally changed people's perception of cruise ship holidays. Previously, most people thought cruising was for those who were not only rich and elderly but, worse still, just plain boring. Well, nine series of top-rating television shows certainly changed all that.

After seeing all the fun and mayhem the show's 'passengers' were getting up to on their cruises, viewers besieged travel agents in their thousands. Even if, up until the first screening of *The Love Boat*, passengers had been inclined to be a trifle sedate, they certainly abandoned all of that after they had seen the programme.

In 1998 she attracted a different kind of publicity after 25kg of heroin was smuggled aboard by crewmen. The discovery was made by Greek police and *Pacific Princess* was impounded while they completed their investigations.

By 2000, she was beginning to show her age, but Princess Cruises knew they had a good thing going and wanted to keep the name alive. They began looking for a more modern replacement. Although *Pacific Princess* was sold in 2001, she was immediately leased back and continued to operate as part of the Princess fleet until in 2002, they bought the Renaissance Cruise Line's *R3* to replace her.

Once the new ship was in their hands, the company promptly repainted *R3* in their house colours and renamed the ship *Pacific Princess*. To keep enjoying the bookings success they had with the original ship, they also gave her the Love Boat mantle. Perhaps the switch went largely unnoticed.

She operated successfully as *Pacific Princess* until 2021, when Princess Cruises sold her to Azamara cruises and she became *Azamara Onward*.

Meanwhile, the first *Pacific Princess* was sold to Pullmantur Cruises of Spain. They simply renamed her MS *Pacific* and sent her back to the Caribbean.

The new *Pacific Princess*. (Author)

From there on, her ownership became a confusing muddle of changing owners and operators. *Pacific* was operated by CVC in Brazil during the southern summer and in 2008, she was chartered by the newly established Quail Cruises to operate cruises out of Valencia, Spain.

That year, *Pacific* was seized by the Italian coastguard for a repair bill owed to a shipyard in Genoa. The Italian authorities decided to sell the ship to pay the debt, but between 2010 and 2011, they held three auctions with no bidders.

In March 2012 the ship was sold for €2.5 million to a Turkish ship-breaking company, but they defaulted on payment. She remained laid up in Genoa until finally in 2013 another Turkish ship breaker stumped up the money and towed her to Aliağa.

In the process of dismantling, there was a flood in a compartment below the engines. Electric pumps were set running and their toxic exhaust gases killed two men and injured nine others.

It was very sad ending for the Love Boat, which had prompted millions around the world to take up cruising.*

---

* The author has written two books on the new *Pacific Princess*: *Pacific Princess: The New Love Boat* (coffee-table book) and *Aboard the Pacific Princess* (two editions, paperback and e-book). For those who want to know more, please visit online booksellers.

31

RMS *Queen Mary*

RMS *Queen Mary*. Final Departure from Southampton to Long Beach. (Author)

Born	1936
Died	Still alive
GRT	80,744
Length	1,019ft
Beam	118ft
Passengers	2,140
Crew	1,100
Line	Cunard Line

Longest-Surviving Liner

Prior to the launch of *Queen Mary*, all Cunard ships had names ending with the letters 'ia'. There was *Caronia, Britannia, Sylvania, Mauretania*, etc. You get the idea. Come 1934, when Cunard began constructing what was billed as the greatest liner ever built, it now made perfect sense for their naming thoughts to turn to Queen Victoria. This was a queen very much revered by her people. She reigned through the Industrial Revolution and died in 1901. They still make movies about her.

But to use the queen's name, Cunard had to win the blessing of the Palace. One of the directors of Cunard, Lord Royden, was a friend of King George V, and was charged by the board to secure the royal consent. When out with the king doing a spot of grouse shooting, as you do, Royden seized his chance.

When the king asked how the building of the new Cunarder was progressing, Royden said it was all going well and the company wanted to name her after 'the most illustrious and remarkable woman who has ever been Queen of England'.

Quick as a flash, the wily king, grandson of Queen Victoria, said, 'That is the greatest compliment ever made to me and my wife. I shall ask her permission when I get home.' His wife, of course, was Queen Mary.

So that was that. Lord Royden was certainly not game enough to cough discreetly and say, 'Actually Sire, I was referring to your grandmother.' So, *Queen Mary* it now was.

Queen Mary could carry 711 first-class passengers, 707 cabin-class passengers and 577 tourist passengers. First-class cabins were opulently furnished, and all had telephones. The suites included a master bedroom, a smaller one for servants or children, a large sitting room and a bathroom. In such a cabin, the trip would cost fifteen times more than a humble cabin in tourist.

On her maiden voyage, fog prevented *Queen Mary* from wresting the coveted Blue Riband for the fastest crossing set by the French liner *Normandie*. Cunard did not want another *Titanic*. Yet one month later, she crossed in three days and twenty-seven minutes at an average speed of 30.14 knots. This shaved five minutes off *Normandie*'s record. The Blue Riband was hers.

In response, *Normandie* opened her throttles and reclaimed it. After a slight modification, *Mary* gained some speed and wrested it back again and then went on to hold it for many years. This was helped by *Normandie*, while berthed in New York City, conveniently bursting into flames. However, Cunard maintained it was not interested in anything as mundane as recording the fastest crossing.

The company claimed their only reason for *Mary* doing a faster run was to give the engines a good work out as a test to help build a sister ship. Oh yeah? But to their credit, Cunard never advertised or promoted the fact it held the record: word of mouth did that.

War Service

Mary was more than halfway to New York when the Second World War was declared. With strong memories of a U-boat's merciless torpedoing of the civilian liner *Lusitania* in the last war, *Mary* sprung into immediate evasive manoeuvres, altering her course to steer a confusing zigzag pattern as she raced to the safety of New York's neutral harbour.

Future scheduled transatlantic crossings were cancelled. She remained tied up in New York with just a skeleton maintenance crew.

Six months later, she was joined by her unfinished sister ship, *Queen Elizabeth*. New York now had the world's two largest liners in its port and tensions were running high. What to do with them? There was some talk of selling the two ships to the Americans, but Winston Churchill had other ideas. Merchant navy ships flying the red ensign flag of Britain could be called up for war service. This was now being done with a vengeance, so why not the Queens?

In the run-up to a possible war, some passenger liners had been built with hulls especially strengthened so they could be heavily armed with warship standard guns. This option for the Queens had been rejected as Britain wanted to indicate the two ships were designed for peace and peace alone. But that had no effect on Hitler; he put a bounty equivalent to £50,000 on the head of each ship.

In those days, that was a very tidy sum of money indeed. For a U-boat commander it would be like winning the national lottery. But with much better odds of a win!

The North Atlantic was known as U-boat Alley. The Queens' captains were very expert seamen, but, nevertheless, as the prized targets for both the German navy and Luftwaffe, it is little short of a miracle they escaped the devastation and sinkings taking place.

The British decided that, risky as it was, the two Queens would make ideal troopships, able to carry whole divisions from one war front to another. The first step was to fit both Queens with antimagnetic coils to protect them against mines. Their speed was their main asset, but as a last-ditch defence, the Queens were also fitted with cannon and anti-aircraft defences.

For conversion to troopships, the two Queens were first sent to Cape Town and, for further work, from there on to Sydney. The first to arrive in Down Under was *Queen Mary*. In her camouflage grey, the locals nicknamed her the Grey Ghost. Despite all the attempts at secrecy, you can't hide a ship of that size in the middle of Sydney. The ship was too big and the harbour too small.

Standing on *Mary*'s bridge, Captain Harry Grattidge heard a local tourist boat announcing over its tannoy speakers, 'On our starboard side, ladies and gents, the greatest phantom you have ever seen. For why? Because you may think it is *Queen Mary* but officially it ain't!'

On another visit to Sydney Harbour, Captain James Bisset took exception to a tug blowing its boilers immediately below *Mary*'s bridge. It was sending up voluminous clouds of sooty black smoke into his immaculate chartroom. Too much for Bisset to take, he grabbed a megaphone, marched to the wing of the bridge and yelled down to the skipper of the tug 80ft below, 'Do that again and I will spit down your funnel and put your bloody fires out.' Some versions of this story say it wasn't spitting that Bisset was threatening to do.

By the spring of 1941, the conversion work was finished and a total of 11,600 Australian soldiers were taken aboard the two ships for transfer to the battle fronts.

Running the Gauntlet

Living in constant fear of being torpedoed, the Queens began their troop transport work. One day, in the middle of a vast and empty ocean, a radio officer rushed up to *Mary*'s bridge, waving a signal and excitedly calling to Captain Bisset that Japanese radio was reporting that *Queen Mary* had just been sunk.

Bisset was calm. He paused, scanned the peaceful horizon thoughtfully, and remarked dryly, 'Better keep it under your hat. Don't tell the troops. It might worry them!'

Neither Queen ever had to fire her guns in anger and instead relied purely on their unmatched speed. However, *Queen Mary* did manage to sink an anti-aircraft cruiser. Unfortunately, it was one of her own.

Mary was approaching the Scottish coast with American troops on board when she picked up her escort fleet to help protect her from the U-boat- and Luftwaffe-infested area ahead. The escort consisted of four Royal Navy destroyers and the anti-aircraft cruiser HMS *Curaçao*.

The flotilla was steaming in zigzag formation when the coded signal went up that zigzag pattern number eight was to be used. This meant *Mary* would turn 25° to starboard and run for eight minutes, then 50° to port and so on with other variations while the escorting flotilla manoeuvred out of the way in pre-planned synchronisation. *Mary* was travelling faster than the flotilla could manage and, essentially, in a few seconds of error, one ship zigged when it should have zagged.

Well, you can guess what happened. *Mary* crashed at full speed into *Curaçao*, slicing her in half and quickly sending her to the bottom. Tragically, on board the cruiser, 329 lives were lost.

To make things worse, *Mary* could not stop. She would have been a sitting target. With an entire division of 15,000 GIs on board, it was far too big a risk to take. Instead, with a gaping hole in her bow, she limped on to Scotland, leaving two navy vessels to pick up the survivors from *Curaçao*.

As troopships, the Queens could, and did, carry up to 15,000 troops and crew. To this day, this still stands as a record for the number of people carried on a single ship. One Queen captain alone, James Bisset, during the war years, transported more than half a million people.

It wasn't comfortable. Both ships were stripped of all their finery and the great public rooms crammed full of makeshift sleeping cots made of stretched canvas. In the high-ceilinged public rooms, the cots could be stacked as high as six tiers. Falling out of the top one was not a good start to the day.

With so many on board, their combined weight could endanger the safety of the ship if she began to roll in a heavy sea. For this reason, the ship was divided into three zones and the troops wore colour-coded badges that strictly confined them to their allotted station.

After consultation with other captains and the British Admiralty, it was decided in winter to reduce the number of troops carried on the North Atlantic run to only 10,000 and only to use the lower bunks.

Once the war was over, the ships were given complete refits and all fittings were replaced so they could perform their normal service. First-class cabins were again opulently furnished. It was interesting to note the first-class suites were mostly occupied by politicians, celebrities, business moguls and, believe it or not, priests. The fact that clergymen were paying so much more than a tourist-class cabin could rankle.

Billy Graham, the skilled evangelist whose oratory talent made it difficult for him to find stadiums big enough for his crusades, was a case in point. Come donation time, he would passionately implore his congregations to give money for Christ. Teams of collectors, carrying large bins, would move through the stadiums collecting cheques and cash while he continued to exhort, 'Don't give change. Give not one dollar, not twenty dollars, nor fifty dollars. Give big. Give until it hurts.' Just the sort of chap you need for a meat raffle down at the pub.

Well, he travelled in a first-class suite. I don't think spending the money hurt him.

The rich and famous were one thing, but the real money-earners on the Queens were the lowly bell boys. Recruited at the age of 15 and invariably cheeky, these smartly uniformed, white-gloved young lads used to run all over the ship paging people for phone calls, opening doors for guests and operating lifts.

Off duty, they slept twelve to a cabin on straw mattresses and were the endless victims of crew hazing. They were stripped and boot polished, locked in cupboards and sent off on fool's errands such as asking the quartermaster for some more green oil for the starboard lamp.

Some initiation ceremonies were totally unacceptable and today would be front-page fodder for the tabloid press for weeks and result in at least three government inquiries. Back then, they just had to shrug it off. But they had the last laugh. They earned phenomenal money in tips.

One bell boy asked the chief steward for a change of job as he felt guilty and that it was not right he was getting so much money. Passengers would press £5 notes into his hand every time he opened a door for them. During the four-and-a-half-day trip he collected £66 in tips.

At the time, that put him on track to nearing what Cunard was paying its captains. This was less than £4,000 a year.

Queen Mary finished her sea duties in 1967 and retired to become a hotel in Long Beach, California. In this role she has had a chequered career with various lease holders running into financial troubles. Through all this, she became neglected, but there is now a dedicated group of US citizens determined that she will be preserved properly for future generations.

There are several *Queen Mary* Facebook groups, but chief among them is QM1 Restore the Queen. You can find them on Facebook or www.qmi.care.

As a former entertainment officer aboard in her dying days, I cannot begin to tell you how heartening it is to see that she still has such a strong and loyal following.

I could write a whole book on the Cunard Queens. Wait a minute, I did! *High Tea on the Cunard Queens* is published by The History Press and in all good bookshops … if you can find one. Alternatively, hop online and get it delivered quickly.

32

SS *United States*

SS *United States*.

Born	1951
Died	Still kicking ... just
GRT	53,330
Length	990ft
Beam	101.5ft
Passengers	1,928
Crew	900
Line	United States Lines

Fastest Across the Atlantic

For decades, the ship breaking the speed record across the Atlantic to New York would win an intangible award known as the Blue Riband. However, no matter how ethereal this prize, it did bring the ship extra passengers, lucrative mail contracts and, for her nation, swelling pride, puffed-up chests and full bragging rights.

The record is based on the highest average speed across the more difficult westbound passage, not the elapsed time as ships departing different ports must follow different routes.

Some commercial venues make various claims to the Blue Ribband name, but I believe the true origin was based on a horse racing prize term rarely used since 1910.

However, in 1935, English politician and shipping magnate Harold Hales thought the title should be recognised with something more tangible. He had an elaborate trophy made and called it the Hales Trophy. Politicians are a modest lot.

While the Hales Trophy lives on to recognise the fastest crossing, it is now held by dubious claimants, such as super high-speed catamarans and the like with no right to claim to be the fastest regular passenger liner on the Atlantic. These are mere spills and thrills merchants out for fame and glory rather than managing the nitty gritty of carrying thousands of passengers safely in all weathers on a regular schedule from the Old World to the New.

Stripped of her former dignity, rusting away in a forgotten dock in a southern Philadelphia parking lot behind an Ikea store, is the former pride of the United States: the last and longest true holder of the Blue Riband. In a sorry state of total neglect, SS *United States*, famous for the marvels of her pioneering technology, streamlined good looks and chic décor, is now in a woeful dilapidated state that is an insult to her name. But she still holds the Blue Riband.

The only possible true challenger of today could be *Queen Mary 2*. But owners Cunard White Star, having won the Blue Riband no fewer than eighteen times with the original *Queen Mary*, holding it for the fourteen years before SS *United States* busted onto the scene, turned up its nose at the mere suggestion of pursuing such an award.

However, at the time of losing the Blue Riband to the new American ship on her maiden voyage, *Queen Mary*'s Captain Gattridge sent his rival captain a note saying, 'Godspeed. Welcome to the Atlantic. Am sacking my chief engineer.'

On her maiden voyage, she notched up an extra 4.5 knots on *Queen Mary*'s record. This caused great jubilation among the crew of *United States*. On arriving in Le Havre, they spotted a British warship moored tightly behind them. Leaning over the taffrail, they called out jaunting and cheering remarks about their victory. Such opportunities are hard for sailors to resist. But the British tars were not to be outdone. Back came the response, 'Get too close to the *Queen Mary* in Southampton and in that little thing you might just get hoisted aboard!'

The top recorded speed of *United States* was 38.32 knots, that's about 45mph. But that wasn't even full power. Her true maximum speed was a closely guarded military secret as she was built in part with US Navy money. It was planned, if necessary, for the ship to be converted within forty-eight hours to a troopship capable of carrying 14,000 soldiers. Fortunately, this need never arose, but passengers would comment on how difficult it was to remain standing on the open deck when she was charging into a strong head wind.

The secret of her speed was twofold. Firstly, she was not of all-steel construction. Although steel was used for the framework, she was clad in much lighter aluminium. Secondly, a lady engineer, unusual for the time, designed a special propulsion system. Her name was Elaine Kaplan and, among other refinements, instead of the usual four-blade propellers she opted for five blades.

Setting Fire to the Piano

The chief designer, William Gibbs, was meticulous in his approach to all aspects of the design and safety of the ship. She had lifeboats galore, far more than her total complement should ever need. And forsaking wood for aluminium all round, the risk of fire was greatly diminished.

Actually, that is not quite true. The fable goes that in the galley, there was a wooden butchers' block and, of course, there was the matter of pianos. Gibbs asked Steinway and Sons to make them out of aluminium. Steinway were appalled and refused to do it, saying the tone would be awful.

Instead, they experimented with fire-resistant mahogany, and they invited Gibbs along to see them set fire to one doused in petrol. The piano didn't burn, and Gibbs let the Steinways aboard.

However, with the ship being built for possible military use, it must be remembered that at high enough temperatures aluminium does in fact burn and melt. When the British ship *Canberra* was requisitioned as a troopship for the Falklands War, considerable amounts of aluminium were removed to reduce the risk of fire.

In the opinion of many, the lack of wood panelling gave the interiors of *United States* a cold and clinical look. This enabled the more stately and homely Cunard ships to hold on to their passengers. However, the rich and famous still flocked to do a glamorous crossing on the new ship and she quickly established herself as the pride of America.

She was relatively late onto the transatlantic scene, some said twenty years or more late, and the rising popularity of air travel was soon licking at her wake. She still had a good share of the summer crossings, but her design was ill-suited for winter cruising and by the 1960s was steaming into financial trouble. Not only had passenger numbers declined, but she was beset with frequent labour disputes and constant fights with the federal government for operating subsidies.

By 1964, her running mate, *America*, was sold off, and for the next five years she was left to run on alone. In 1969, she notched up the completion of her 400th voyage and was sent to the shipyard for a refit. However, she was never to re-emerge. United States Lines decided she was no longer viable and her seventeen-year career came to an end without a grand send-off, or even much of a whimper.

Now the trouble started. Suitors were sought to buy her but deal after deal collapsed. Not helping matters was the fact that the United States Government was reluctant to let her go to some, due to her potential use as a troopship that could end up working against the United States.

The work carried out on board did not help matters either. The vessel was also listed on the National Register of Historic Places as having 'compelling national significance', a status earned by fewer than 1 per cent of the 90,000 listed US historic properties.

However, this proved of little use as first her furnishings were auctioned and then the belated discovery of just how damaging asbestos can be to health led to the removal of all her linings, which Gibbs had installed due to his preoccupation with avoiding fire at sea. In short, she was gutted and was becoming a proposition no company was prepared to take on.

By 2010 she seemed sure to be sent to the scrapyards, but a last-minute rescue came with a large donation from a local billionaire to fund the formation of the SS United States Conservancy. This was then able to take ownership of the vessel.

The conservancy was headed up by Susan Gibbs, the granddaughter of William Gibbs, the ship's chief designer. She has brought hard work and dedication to ensuring SS *United States* is preserved for posterity. However, their working funds struggle to even cover the cost of her berthing and compulsory insurance.

You could hardly call it life support as her condition has continued to deteriorate. But while pundits on social media continue to lament her pathetic state, the Conservancy still has faith.

In 2020, a leading New York developer, RXR Reality, partnered with the Conservancy in a new bid to find a permanent home in a United States city. The ship in now being pitched as a permanently moored floating structure offering a museum, a hotel and 'a collection of hospitality and cultural spaces to serve as a new contemporary centrepiece for their waterfronts'. Targeted cities include Boston, New York, Philadelphia, Miami, Seattle, San Francisco, Los Angeles and San Diego.

Two years later, there have been no developments to report, but on the other hand it has been a time of huge economic and cultural upheaval due to the Covid-19 pandemic.

Susan Gibbs and the conservancy claim the once-grand old ship is 'a survivor' and that they are not done yet. The struggle to preserve her continues.

33

HMY *Britannia*

HMY *Britannia*. (Courtesy of © Marc Millar)

Born	1954
Died	Still kicking
GRT	5,769
Length	412ft
Beam	55ft
Passengers	250
Crew	271

Cruising with the Royals

'Welcome aboard, Your Highness.' This was the likely greeting when stepping aboard the Royal Yacht *Britannia*. Either that or you had to be good mates with one of the royals or serving in the Royal Navy. I don't really know; I never got the invite.

However, now she is open to all, and we can board for the sum of £18. We can even see the Queen's Stateroom, but there can be no jumping on the bed as this room is behind glass. And we're not going anywhere as this former pride of the British royalty has taken up permanent residence in Edinburgh. Her long days of cruising the Commonwealth and waving the British flag may be over, but she is still attracting more than 300,000 visits a year.

She was not the first royal yacht on the scene. In fact, she was the eighty-third since 1660, when the bewigged and ribbon-bedecked Charles II first took to the seas in ruffled petticoat breeches.

Britannia was the first royal yacht not powered by sail. Her immediate predecessor, the eponymously named *Victoria & Albert III*, was built for Queen Victoria. However, this queen was not amused and never set foot aboard, fearing yachts to be tippy things. Her Royal Highness considered being on horseback safer and more stable. To each their own. However, her ship proved a real workhorse, serving four sovereigns for more than thirty-eight years.

Britain now felt it needed a royal yacht capable of cruising anywhere in the world, while serving as a royal residence suitable for holding receptions for presidents and prime ministers. In times of war, she could also serve as a hospital ship and in the event of the much-feared nuclear holocaust, she would be off to the north-west coast of Scotland as a place of refuge for the royal family.

The famous Scottish shipyard of John Brown, builder of both *Queen Mary* and *Queen Elizabeth*, was commissioned to construct the new ship. She was to be the last of their fully riveted ships, but the hull finish was the smoothest ever achieved. It seems it is possible to conceal all those lumpy rivet heads edging the steel plates.

It was also hoped *Britannia* would serve as a convalescence cruise ship for King George VI's ailing health, but he passed away two days after the order for the new ship was placed.

Kindergarten at Sea

It fell in 1953 to his daughter, Queen Elizabeth, to christen the new ship. A year later, *Britannia* was off on her first mission to Malta, with Princess Anne and Prince Charles on board ready to be reunited with their mum and dad at the end of the royal couple's Commonwealth Tour.

Royal duty milk was important for the royal children and the first royal duty for the captain was to meet a farmer's wife who provided her very best thirty-day supply of milk to go into the ship's cool room. The wife then put a similar amount into storage at her farm. She checked its keeping properties by drinking a pint every day to see if it was still perfect. If she had keeled over, they would have sent an urgent telex to the ship saying, 'Don't drink the milk!'

More than 1,000 Royal Navy personnel applied to crew the royal yacht. Officers could serve for two years. The 272 selected crew were called 'yachtsmen' and, if they served with an unblemished record, they could stay on the royal yacht until their retirement.

Unlike other naval ships, with their constant blowing of whistles and barked commands, the running of *Britannia* was done in complete silence. Anyone who has ever done a Mediterranean cruise with announcements in five different languages can imagine what complete and utter bliss this would be. It would be quieter than that dreadful involuntary pause when your partner asks, 'Do I look fat in this?'

On *Britannia*, there were no bugle calls and below decks the crew whispered into strategically placed telephones. Above decks, all officers were proficient in semaphore and, to direct the crew, they silently waved colour-coded paddles.

A Life of Duty

During the ship's career, the queen entertained on board US Presidents Dwight D. Eisenhower, Gerald Ford, Ronald Reagan and Bill Clinton.

For the royal family, *Britannia*, with her accompanying protective destroyer, was an ideal secure honeymoon venue. Those using her for this purpose included Princess Margaret and Antony Armstrong-Jones and Charles and Diana. Erm, maybe not such a good record there.

As a young lad, I often sailed with my brother in our small boat to the famous Cowes Week regatta. Nearly always there was *Britannia* and her escorting Royal Navy warship, moored to watch the racing and serve as somewhere for Prince Philip to hop aboard for a warming shower after racing his keel boat *Bloodhound*.

Less glamorous was the egalitarian use of the ship to evacuate 1,000 British nationals trapped by the civil war in Aden in 1986. In a similar vein, her final foreign mission was to bring back the Prince of Wales and the last Governor of Hong Kong, Chris Patten, from Hong Kong after its handover to the People's Republic of China in 1997.

It was a double whammy for Britannia ruling the waves as later the same year, politics entered the fore, and it was determined *Britannia* had to go. After forty-four years, a major refit was needed. It was projected to cost £17 million. The ship was run and paid for by the British Government. After all, that was who the royal family was working for.

The royal family are the country's leading ambassadors and used *Britannia* to promote trade and industry around the globe. The Overseas Trade Board estimated that £3 billion was made for the Exchequer from commercial days on *Britannia* between 1991 and 1995 alone.

OK, the royal family had occasional personal use of the ship, but surely, this was not all that different from taking the company car home at the weekends.

The politics of envy reared its ugly head. The Tories wanted to go ahead and order a new ship. The Labour opposition said it was not ready to commit the people's money to such an elitist project and perhaps if the queen wanted a royal yacht, she should go and buy one herself.

To the queen, that must have been like being asked to pay for that company car. She was not as rich as people tend to think. Most of her assets were tied up, belonging to her country. She was not even the richest lady in England; writing Harry Potter books brings more money. Wisely, the queen kept out of it and said she was quite happy to do her duties by plane.

Britannia was decommissioned in December 1997. Overall, *Britannia* carried the queen and various other dignitaries on 696 foreign visits, 272 home visits and travelled more than a million miles in high security and at relatively little cost.

The queen worked for Britain tirelessly, and while visiting far-flung lands, *Britannia* offered her somewhere quiet and secure to come home to, put her feet up and enjoy a nice cup of tea. Small wonder that at the decommissioning ceremony, the normally stoic queen was seen to sneakily shed a tear.

Today, the clocks on board are permanently stopped at 3.01, the time the queen last disembarked.

34

RMS *Queen Elizabeth 2*

RMS *Queen Elizabeth 2* (QE2). (Author)

Born	1969
Died	Still kicking
GRT	65.863
Length	963ft
Beam	105ft
Passengers	1,777
Crew	1,040
Line	Cunard Line

The Most-Travelled Liner

Early in the 1960s, it was becoming very apparent to the Cunard board that the Atlantic crossing trade was dwindling and her two reliable old workhorses, *Queen Mary* and *Queen Elizabeth*, were coming to the end of their lives. They set about designing a smaller ship that was less expensive to run and easily adaptable to cruising.

For this, it decided on two-class segregation, but by horizontal division, rather than vertical and the ship must be able to pass through the Suez and Panama canals. They still needed the new ship to travel the Atlantic at the same fast speed as the Queens, but she had to consume far less oil and be able to travel 8,000 miles without bunkering.

This also called for a distillation plant to convert the sea into drinking water, making the liner almost self-sufficient. For Atlantic crossings, the ship would operate with two classes but for cruising she would convert to a one-class ship. Thus, with a profile more reminiscent of a super yacht than a traditional liner, the design for *QE2* was born.

Out on the builder's slipway, the riveting together of steel plates had been replaced by welding and large parts of the superstructure were built of aluminium. The lack of riveting might have been a boon to shipbuilders, but it was the end of some sailor's favourite sport. On various nationality ships I worked on, officers chatting up young ladies at the bar would ask girls to guess the number of rivets it took to build the ship. In the case of *Mary*, it was 10 million.

The girls would be impressed. They were then asked if they knew the last rivet punched into the ship was ceremonially marked by using one made of solid gold? Would they like to see it? Of course, they would. Luckily, it was in the officer's cabin. Really?

I should mention that on one Greek ship I worked on there were no fewer than eight golden rivets! They were a dab hand with a spot of gold paint.

With this enticement, many a probably suspecting damsel would happily go to see the golden rivet. However, there are no such rivets to be found in the hull of most new ships. Ladies: forewarned is forearmed.

The new ship was completed in 1969 and with the same gold scissors used first by her grandmother for the launch of *Mary* and then by her mother for *Elizabeth*, Queen Elizabeth II cut the ribbon and launched both ship and herself into another royal naming controversy.

In the sealed envelope given to the queen on her arrival, the card simply said, 'I name this ship Queen Elizabeth.' But on the launch platform, Queen Elizabeth left the nomination envelope unopened and instead said, 'I name this ship Queen Elizabeth the Second.' In other words, intentionally or not, she appeared to have named it after herself. Queens can do that sort of thing.

Following this shock, after the queen pressed the electronic launch button, the ship didn't budge. It just sat on the slipway.

This is a very bad omen for superstitious seamen. In reality, it was only for a few moments, but it must have felt like eternity. Into the stony silence, a workman on the ship's foredeck called down, 'Give us a shove!'

On the slipway and playing the crowd for humour, the shipyard director, suited and bowler-hatted, made to move the massive ship by doing just that. As he did, the ship began to move. Wow. But it was a coincidence, of course.

Queen Elizabeth the Second is not the shortest name for a ship and although the hull was plenty long enough, writing it on the sides called for new graphics. Both *Queen Mary* and *Queen Elizabeth* had their names on the bow and stern in block capital letters. This time Cunard opted for upper and lower case and instead of the normal Roman numeral II, Cunard used the Arabic numeral 2.

This was a somewhat confusing move at the time, but it was an attempt to remove the ship from being named after Queen Elizabeth II. The problem was the ship had been built in Scotland and in that country, Queen Elizabeth II was only their Queen Elizabeth I. And heaven help any Englishman that ever inferred anything else. Mercifully, the Queen Elizabeth 2 dilemma was quickly solved as she became popularly known as *QE2*.

With all fitting out finished, she entered service in 1969. It was a big year for travel: the Concorde supersonic jet was unveiled, and Apollo 11 blasted off for the first successful manned Moon landing. 'One small step for man, one giant leap for Cunard.'

With her sleek, futuristic looks, *QE2* fitted right in as a child of her era. There were some technical teething problems, but slow-to-accept, crusty seafarers were surprised to see how quickly she assumed the majestic mantle of reverence worn by the previous Queens.

Perils at Sea

She was often in the news. In 1971, she promptly answered a Mayday call from the French cruise ship *Antilles*, which hit a reef off the Caribbean Island of Mustique, ruptured her oil tanks and then burst into flames. Five hundred passengers took to the lifeboats to land on a nearby beach before being tendered to *QE2*. One *Antilles* passenger claimed that the ship swap was worth it.

In 1974 she came to the rescue of six yachties in the Mediterranean and took them off their sinking sailing boat.

In 1990, she was called to rescue the forty-nine crew members of a sinking oil rig that had broken loose while being towed in an 80mph storm in the North Sea. With the weather easing, the oil rig crew forsook the luxury on offer from the world's most famous liner and opted to stay on their imperilled oil rig. It was a poor choice. After *QE2* sailed on, the rig did capsize. Fortunately, no lives were lost.

A year later, when 1,000 miles from New York and on passage to Southampton, the company's New York office received a ransom note saying there were six bombs on board and set to explode unless a demand of $350,000 was met. With the ship at a stop in mid-ocean and under the watchful eyes of 1,500 disconcerted passengers and crew, a scrambled British Special Air Services bomb disposal team parachuted into the sea near the ship. They were picked up in lifeboats and brought aboard to help conduct a full search. This was a bit of excitement not found on your average cruise.

However, not a single bomb was found. Did this make the passengers happy? No, now they were even more anxious. Where were those bombs?

There was no big bang: the extortionist had been bluffing. This story ends with the FBI getting their man and his being sentenced to twenty years in jail. That would teach him not to mess with a Queen.

The following year, Muammar Gaddafi hatched a plan to send a submarine to torpedo *QE2* while she was on a cruise off the coast of Israel. Gaddafi was seeking revenge for Israel's downing of Libyan Flight 114.

Although Cunard had increased security for these waters, passengers were happily partying the cruise away and unaware of the planned attack. Fortunately, Egyptian President Anwar Sadat was not unaware of what Gaddafi was up to as it was one of his submarines Gaddafi was using. He countermanded the order and *QE2* was spared. Thus, the ship fared better than Gaddafi as, of course, he was himself later assassinated.

Even in dry dock the ship was not safe from threats. In 1976, the IRA attempted to blow up the ship. Three men were arrested and sentenced to twenty years.

It's War

The British territories of the Falklands are among the least desirable places in the world to live. Wave-battered and 1,500 miles off the Argentinian coast, they are cold, bleak and lonely. South Georgia and the South Sandwich Islands have not one permanent resident. The only population is on the Falkland Islands, where there are 1,820 proud-to-be-British citizens and 400,000 sheep of unknown nationality preference.

By virtue of proximity, the Argentinians think these islands should be theirs. Why anyone would want them, heaven knows, but to divert attention from its failing home economic policies, the troubled military government invaded the islands in 1982 and took possession.

Of course, they knew Britain wouldn't like it, but what the heck was she going to do about it? After all, the United Kingdom was 8,000 miles away.

But they had not counted on Britain's first female prime minister, Margaret Thatcher. She was not called the Iron Lady for nothing, and besides, with the strike trouble she was having in Britain, she was quite glad of a little political diversion herself.

So, act they did. The British immediately put together an invasion fleet of no fewer than 127 ships. This armada consisted of sixty-five naval vessels and sixty-two requisitioned merchant ships. It was a huge task but done in a few weeks and look out, here we come. However, to us back home, brought up thinking the next war would be all about atomic bombs and nuclear fallout shelters and all over in ten minutes, it seemed as though time was standing still.

To the world's surprise, the British Government conscripted as troop-ships its two most valuable liners, *QE2* and P&O's *Canberra*. Cruises were cancelled, and passengers were left standing with their luggage on the pier and nowhere to go.

This was no Mickey Mouse war. Seven ships were sunk, nearly 200 air-craft destroyed, thousands wounded, and more than 900 lives lost:

649 Argentine military, 255 British military and three Falkland Islanders. Hardly the safest place for Britain to send her most valued liner.

In just nine days at Southampton, *QE2* was prepared for war. The top decks of the stern were sliced off, pools decked over and the forward quarter deck extended over the capstans to create helicopter landing pads. Fuel pipes were fitted for refuelling at sea.

Steel plate was used to reinforce the ship for a quarter of her length and an antimagnetic coil added to protect against the menace of naval mines. Thoughtfully, extra life jackets were also put on.

The ship's 12 miles of luxury carpeting were covered with 2,000 sheets of hardboard. Valuable soft furnishings, paintings and five grand pianos were deemed 'not for the use of troops' and taken ashore for safe storage. Finally, the public lounges were converted into dormitories and the formerly luxurious *QE2* was a warship.

With Argentinian submarines and aircraft out looking for her, the blacked-out and camouflaged-painted *QE2* zigzagged for eighteen days on her way to South Georgia.

With the troops delivered, *QE2*'s job was nearly done. On her return trip she became a hospital ship and carried home more than 600 of the wounded. Arriving back in Southampton, it took nine weeks and several million pounds to restore *QE2* to her former glory before she could resume her weekly five-day transatlantic crossings.

So, again she became another Queen that escaped the conflict unharmed.

Facing the Seas

No ship goes through thirty-nine years of world cruising and Atlantic crossings without encountering the odd spot of bother with the weather.

In 1976 a very rough sea caused a 12½-ton anchor to break loose and punch a hole in her bulbous bow. She began to take in water but, with the pumps working flat out, she made it into Boston for repairs.

She was caught in a big Atlantic hurricane in 1978 but the real horror came in 1995 when she had to heave to in the face of 120-knot winds from Hurricane Louis, 200 miles off the coast of Newfoundland. The seas were running at 40–50ft when up came a rogue wave estimated at 90ft.

According to Captain Warwick, the seething mass of water was like looking at the White Cliffs of Dover. The weight of the water crashing onto the foredeck dented deck plating and bent some of the rails. But all was calm on board.

On another occasion, with *QE2* hove to for nearly twenty-four hours in 100mph winds, Captain Arnott wished to give an impression of calm to his passengers by joining them for dinner in the dining room. Just as he entered, the ship gave a terrific lurch and diners, chairs and crockery went everywhere. The captain braced himself. His instinct was to run to the bridge to check what was happening, but instead, when the ship settled, he proceeded calmly to his table. He was imagining the panic in the dining room if he had turned and fled back to the bridge.

Keeping Up Appearances

With a career stretching over thirty-nine years, a lady must be kept in the best possible condition, and this needs occasional visits to the beauty parlour. In 1998 she went for her biggest update: a $30 million makeover resulting from a major cash injection from the US-based Carnival Corporation that was taking over Cunard. The hull was stripped to bare metal and she was repainted in black with a white superstructure. Once more, *QE2* could look in the mirror and claim to be the 'fairest of them all'.

In 2004 the transatlantic run was assigned to Cunard's new flagship, *Queen Mary 2*, and *QE2* switched to full-time cruising.

Faced with the expense of meeting some of Britain's strict new legal port restrictions, in November 2008, Cunard retired *QE2*. A Dubai company trumped up $100 million.

This made Beatrice Muller, an elderly widow passenger who lived mostly in her cabin on the ship for ten years, homeless. She regarded it her permanent home and considered her $100,000 a year travel bill as 'rent money'.

Dubai's original plan was to keep *QE2* in seaworthy condition and use her as a 500-room hotel ship and tourist attraction at the luxury Palm Jumeirah complex. The only alteration to the ship before leaving for Dubai was the careful removal of the synagogue. Dubai didn't seem to think they would have a use for that. In fact, in her entire career, the synagogue was the only room on the ship never altered.

She arrived in Dubai to the cheers of onlookers, fireworks, a welcoming crowd of thousands and an Emirates jet fly past. But the party was short-lived as at the same time the world financial markets collapsed.

The Dubai company found itself in the unenviable position of not having the money to complete the conversion and not being able to sell her. Cunard had inserted a clause in the sales contract that stipulated there could be no onward sale for ten years without payment of another $100 million.

After a long period in limbo, *QE2* is now open and operating as a first-class hotel in Dubai. *QE2* sailed for just short of forty years and at that point was the longest-serving Queen in Cunard history. She voyaged 5.6 million miles and carried 2.5 million passengers on 806 transatlantic crossings. Name me a ship that can top that.

35

RMS *Queen Mary 2*

RMS *Queen Mary 2* (*QM2*). (Author)

Born	2004
Died	Still cruising
GRT	149,215
Length	1,132ft
Beam	135ft
Passengers	2,695
Crew	1,253
Line	Cunard Line

The Ship That Would Never Happen

It is thirty-seven years since I worked on the first *Queen Mary* as an entertainment officer on her final transatlantic from New York. It was the end of an era. It was predicted that never again would there be a great ocean liner. Yet here I am, standing high on the uppermost deck of the new *Queen Mary 2*, about to depart Southampton on her maiden voyage. Only this time Cunard is not paying me. I am paying them.

And it's worth it. As the lines are cast off, a continual barrage of fireworks flares into the night sky, flooding the huge ship in a myriad of disco hues. The deafening roar of the ship's whistles joins the cacophony of explosions and the rousing rendition of 'Rule Britannia' blasting from the ship's speakers.

Looking up, I recognise one of the ¾-ton, 7ft steam whistles. I should do. I had sailed under it before when it was on the original *Queen Mary's* middle stack. Its resounding boom carries for 10 miles. It has been shipped over from Long Beach on *QE2* to sail the seas once more.

They were wrong that the 1960s had seen the end of the great ocean liners. We are here on the largest, longest, tallest, widest and most expensive liner ever built.

How could such a ship come into being? Well, we are now ten days into our run and the man who knows the story better than anyone is standing beside me at the rail as we watch dawn breaking over the Caribbean Island of St Thomas.

He is the designer and project manager of *QM2*, and we are taking a critical look at the cruise ship, *Venture of the Seas*, from rival cruise company, Royal Caribbean. She is anchoring beside us in the bay off Charlotte Amalie. He is telling me that until we arrived, she was the largest ship in the world, but that company is already planning to build a ship bigger than the one we are on.

As we are still on our maiden voyage, I express some horror and sympathy that *QM2* is to have such a short reign as the largest ship. He shrugs, then grins and says, 'But their new one won't be a liner. This is a real ship!'

And there's the big difference. A liner is a real ship, capable of keeping a schedule across the rough winter seas of the North Atlantic. To breast the huge waves requires a high, long, narrow, sheer and reinforced bow that takes up nearly a third of the ship.

This design does away with many of the high-revenue, balcony cabins from the forward part of the vessel. For longevity and strength, steel, not aluminium, must be used. Compounding matters, the heavy weight of steel does away with the ability to build a complete deck of cabins. All this adds about 40 per cent to the costs. This is definitely an expense arena few cruise companies wish to enter.

But this quiet man beside me has managed to talk his hard-bitten employers into this high-risk, $780 million venture. He is a man of modest demeanour, but with a true fairy story so incredible it would even challenge the imagination of Hans Christian Andersen. For this is Stephen Payne, the driving force behind the creation of this amazing new ship.

Born in 1960, Payne's obsession with ships began at age 5 when he was watching the BBC children's television show *Blue Peter*. They were showing a film of QE2, and young Stephen was fascinated. Four years later, he persuaded his family to take him to Southampton Docks, where he could see the liner for himself.

At age 12, Stephen was still watching *Blue Peter* and the programme was now showing film of *Queen Elizabeth* on fire in Hong Kong. The voiceover was saying nothing like her would ever be built again. Young Stephen was horrified and sent off a protest letter to say they were wrong and another ship to rival her would indeed be built and he was the person who was going to design her. Here were his plans and suggestions to prove it.

The programme sent their special Blue Peter badge and, while congratulating him on his ambition, cautioned him not to be discouraged if it never happened. But happen it did. And yes, it was Stephen who designed her.

The badge arrived but it was just the standard one. Young Stephen was disappointed. He thought his efforts had warranted the gold badge. Miffed but undeterred, he went on to finish school and enrol in the University of Southampton's Ship Science programme.

After graduating with a BSc (Hons) in Ship Science, he commenced a successful ship-designing career. This resulted in him landing a job at Carnival, one of the world's biggest operators of cruise lines, and now the owners of Cunard.

The boss of Carnival, Mickey Arison, had seen the movie *Titanic* and noted the huge wave of nostalgia it developed for the days of the great ocean liners. Thus inspired, Carnival liked the idea of introducing to the world another great ocean liner. And among their design team, Arison had just the man for the job: Stephen Payne.

Stephen was passionate in his design approach. Having a thorough appreciation of the history of the early liners, he set out to create a ship with all the majesty of the past, but with the ability to meet modern cruising needs.

On the day before the naming ceremony, *Blue Peter* sent a camera crew to film this extraordinary story. After being given a tour of the ship by Stephen, the programme finally gave him his gold badge.

QM2's speed of 30 knots is twice the speed of the average Caribbean cruise ship. Powering the liner along are four pods that hang beneath the waterline like outboard motors. Each one weighs more than a fully loaded jumbo jet. And yet this monster floats.

There are no rock-climbing walls, dodgem cars or ice rinks on *QM2*. This is a Cunarder: that means she is a very classy ship. Of all things, there is a massive planetarium on board. You don't even need to go up on deck to look at the stars.

The building of this magnificent liner resulted in one tragedy. During the final stages of fitting out there were 2,600 workers boarding and leaving daily across gangways. Just before leaving for sea trials, the yard management decided to treat their workers by letting them bring family and friends for a visit. This meant they would have to handle a lot more people.

To facilitate this, it was decided to install a new gangway just under half a metre wider than the one previously being used. The next day, tragedy struck. With forty-eight people on it, 20m above the concrete floor of the dry dock, it collapsed. Fifteen people were killed and thirty-two were injured.

Out of respect, work was halted, and sea trials were delayed. However, when held, they were successful and, along with *QE2*, Cunard now had the two fastest ocean liners in the world.

For her maiden voyage, in command is Commodore Ronald Warwick, son of former *QE2* Commodore Bil Warwick, who commanded the *QE2*'s maiden voyage thirty-five years before. Yes, that's right, there is only one 'l' in Bil, He was even more economical with his crew. On *QE2* he had 1,000 crew members. Son Ronald has a crew of 250 more: the largest crew ever assembled for a passenger ship at the time.

The fourteen-day cruise taking her to Fort Lauderdale calls at Madeira, Tenerife, Las Palmas, Barbados and St Thomas. At lifeboat drill, I discover that, if things go wrong, we will be sharing a lifeboat with Welsh songstress Dame Shirley Bassey. This is along with a disconcertingly large crowd of others.

Ah well, we console ourselves, if the ship goes down, in our lifeboat we can at least go out with a song.

At sea and in the Bay of Biscay, we hit 6m waves and a full gale with gusts reaching 70mph. Not the best start, but the ship is surprisingly stable. One bonus is that at lunchtime the massive two-decked Britannia Restaurant is virtually empty. Which is just as well, as many of the new waiters have also been knocked off their feet.

Each arrival of *Queen Mary 2* in the European ports is met with spectacular displays from fire boats shooting coloured spumes of water high into the air and huge welcoming crowds at the docks. With news helicopters hovering overhead, the ports maintain full carnival mode all day before sending her off in the evening with another spectacular firework display. It is the stateliest and most celebrated reception any ship has ever received.

The best is saved to last as she receives a spectacular greeting on arrival at Fort Lauderdale with live television coverage on all major networks. Thousands crowd the vantage points at the port entrance.

Everywhere, security is very tight. US Navy and Coastguard patrol boats with flashing blue lights keep spectator boats at bay, while snipers keep a protective watch from rooftops.

As soon as we dock, an underwater security net is positioned a few yards off from the ship and then patrolled by armed security vessels. This is to prevent any chance of a frogmen attack. Up in the sky, a no-fly zone protects the airspace over the ship.

The al-Qaeda attack on the Twin Towers in 2001 hit the holiday industry hard. Now newspaper reports were saying the terrorist organisation, in its Jihad against the West, was threatening to target luxury liners and specifically mentioned *QM2*'s maiden voyage.

A US spy plane discovered scores of acoustic sea mines had disappeared from a naval base in North Korea and US intelligence services feared they could be on board terror ships assembled by Osama bin Laden. The mines were fitted with homing devices that allowed them to zero in on large targets. And they didn't come any larger than *Queen Mary 2*.

When al-Qaeda's chief of naval operations, Al-Neshari, was captured he was carrying a large dossier listing many big cruise liners in Western ports as 'targets of opportunity'. Fortunately, so far, there have been few incidents involving cruise ships.

After ten years, *QM2* can proudly boast she is the largest single consumer of Russian caviar in the history of the entire world: 11,830 kilos of the stuff. This has been washed down with 1.2 million bottles of champagne, and, of course to prove her British credentials, more than 21 million cups of tea.

She has had several refits to keep her in tip-top condition, and when I sailed on her in 2020, I found her looking as fresh and exciting as she had on her maiden voyage and ready to give many more years of service.

But on that trip, the advent of Covid-19 meant popular Captain Aseem Hashmi was forced to leave all his passengers, including me, in Perth in March 2020. He took the ship straight back to England with minimal people on board. Covid-19 kept *QM2* out of service for nearly two years, but once the travel ban was lifted, her loyal passengers quickly returned.

36

Oasis Class of Sisters

Allure of the Seas, an Oasis-class ship. (Author)

Wonder of the Seas Born	2022
Died	Still cruising
GRT	236,857
Length	1,187ft
Beam	210ft
Passengers	6,988
Crew	2,300
Line	Royal Caribbean
Sister ships	*Oasis of the Seas, Allure of the Seas, Harmony of the Seas* and *Symphony of the Seas*

The World's Biggest Cruise Ships

Imagine designing an entire small city, all at once. Then imagine that city not only has to float, but to cruise at upwards of 20 knots while providing a great vacation experience for more than 5,400 guests. And then remember this must be done for every single day of every single week. Furthermore, there can be no costly downtime for port turnarounds.

This was the challenge Royal Caribbean faced when planning *Oasis of the Seas*. The company brought together the largest creative shipping team ever assembled. It consisted of thirty-seven design firms, twenty architectural companies, 130 members of Royal Caribbean's own building and design group and an equally large staff of architects and engineers from the builder's shipyard.

It was a humongous project, requiring between 9 to 10 million working hours for design and construction. It was known as 'Project Genesis'. It gradually honed the concept into the creation of special neighbourhood areas within the vessel and introduced a dramatic split superstructure to allow daylight to flood right down into the centre of the ship.

Each of the two initial ships ordered, *Oasis of the Seas* and *Allure of the Seas*, cost $1.4 billion. They were as long as four football pitches, wider than the wingspan of a Boeing 747 jumbo jet and took up as much space as five jumbos lined up head to tail on a runway – not an unfamiliar sight to those flying out of Chicago.

Although it was originally only planned to build two, their instant success made the line take the total to five. The first to arrive was *Oasis of the Seas*. Launched in 2009, she weighed in at 225,282 tons and was 1,178ft long, 213ft wide and could carry 6,296 passengers. Close on her heels and in the following year, came *Allure of the Seas*. But, although she was conceived, specified and built as an identical ship, something had gone wrong. Both ships had an identical tonnage, but at the time of her official measuring she came in at nearly 2in longer than *Oasis*.

This was not planned and was put down to metal temperature variations during the building or measuring phase. But it put the cat among the pigeons between the crews of the world's two largest cruise ships. Somewhat to the chagrin of *Oasis*, *Allure* promptly laid claim to the title of being the largest cruise ship ever built.

But in turn, her reign was to be short-lived. Rather than see its two sisters squabbling over the title, Royal Caribbean settled the dispute by ordering yet another ship. This was planned to be a whole 2ft longer than *Allure*. So there.

Launched in 2016, this third ship, *Harmony of the Seas*, lifted the tonnage by 1,718 gross tons. However, as both the crews of *Allure* and *Oasis* are quick to point out, she carries fewer passengers. Royal Caribbean continued to build more ships in the Oasis class. *Symphony of the Seas* was delivered in 2018, of course, a bit bigger again, and then in 2022 the fifth and biggest of all in the Oasis class, *Wonder of the Seas*.

At a cost of $7 billion, on any given day on various seas, there can be nearly 50,000 people living in a special Oasis world entirely created by the visionaries at Royal Caribbean.

How Good is Big?

Why build the largest ships in the world? What does it mean for passengers? True comfort on a cruise ship depends on two main factors: the passenger space ratio and the number of crew to service each individual passenger. The gross registered tonnage is a figure calculated to measure the internal volume of a ship, not its weight. So, to work out the passenger space ratio, you divide the tonnage by the average number of passengers. You can see that when you start with 225,000 tons, you have lots of room to play with.

And it's the same with the service. You simply divide the number of passengers by the number of crew and you get an indication of the level of service. Added to this, an intelligent new design approach and good crew training has ensured that everything has been scaled up to make for maximum comfort on board an Oasis-class ship.

Early proof of this is found when you board and when you disembark. Because everything has been so well designed and managed, these procedures on an Oasis ship are among the fastest found on ships. On the first day of boarding you can be from taxi kerb to being shown your stateroom in fifteen minutes. Even the smallest can have trouble equalling that.

There are many other benefits of being on the mega-sized Oasis class. There is the sheer variety of everything: the wide scope of entertainment, the different types of bars and the great choice of restaurants. You can choose between going for a stroll in the park or sitting with a book in the peaceful privacy of your own balcony.

However, if you meet some people you want to see again, you should exchange contact details. Otherwise, you can go the whole trip and not find them. So, oddly enough, if you so desire, the vastness of the ship can make for more privacy.

The Oasis-class ships are designed to appeal to families. To prevent crowding while keeping passengers busy all day, the ships have been divided into seven themed neighbourhoods. They are:

The Boardwalk, home to an amphitheatre-style pool, a full-size carousel, and rock-climbing walls.

The Pool and Sports Zone, with FlowRider surf simulators, a zip line, nine-hole miniature golf course and courts for basketball, volleyball and soccer.

Central Park area, an amazing peaceful place in the centre of the ship, featuring lush plants and winding pathways leading to quiet nooks.

The Royal Promenade, bustling with parades, theme parties, eateries, retail shops and bars and lounges.

Entertainment Place, which can have features such as glow-in-the-dark laser tag battles, ice skating, bumper car rinks and theatres.

Wonder of the Seas is the fifth cruise ship of Royal Caribbean's Oasis class and is nearly 5 per cent larger than the first. It has more than twenty restaurants and bars and amenities including surf simulators, the tallest water slide at sea, zip line, rock climbing walls and an open-air park with 20,000 plants. (Courtesy of © Royal Caribbean)

A Youth Zone with spaces and activities designed to keep the kids happy and out of your hair.

And the Vitality Spa and Fitness zone, which has a beauty salon and barber shop and a fitness centre.

Of course, all this is not everybody's idea of cruising but the sheer size of it all takes the breath away.

An Unusual Captain

On *Allure of the Seas*, I meet Captain Johnny and explain that in the 1960s I too used to work on the biggest ship in the world. I concede that I suspect his might be a bit bigger. In fact, it is nearly three times the size.

Captain Johnny Faevelen is a very unusual captain. He is sitting on an electric motorcycle with his pet parrot perched on his shoulder. I admire the motorcycle, but he is quick to point out that he also has a Harley on board. That, I gather is more for runs on shore, but he uses the electric motorcycle to get about his ship. It can even be used to get from one wing of the bridge to the other, which is 215ft across. But mostly he uses it to cruise along I-95.

This is the crew name for the internal corridor running the full length of the ship and is out of sight of the passengers. With separate lanes for motorised vehicles and pedestrians, this hidden service corridor bustles with traffic. It is very aptly named after the USA's busiest highway, although many claim that as crew come from so many different nationalities it is named after the USA immigration form.

Captain Johnny, as he is known to his passengers, makes a weekly inspection of every aspect of the ship and the motorcycle is just what he needs to get around. On other days, he is out and about talking to passengers.

He will tell you that *Allure* uses 600,000 gallons every day and carries plenty of reserve fuel. In fact, the ship carries enough fuel to take the ship from Miami to Europe and back again. On a normal cruise schedule, refuelling takes place every fourteen days.

Captain Johnny is extremely proud of his ship's stability. Due to its wide beam, it gives an extremely smooth ride, even in rough seas. As soon as the ship tilts a mere half of one degree, the stabilisers are deployed. This is in stark contrast to some ships, which, to save fuel costs, only deploy their stabilisers when the ship has already started to roll. And once such a ship really begins to roll, putting out the stabilisers a little too late has a lessened and delayed effect.

For such a huge ship, the Oasis class is surprisingly manoeuvrable. Once Captain Johnny demonstrated this to another ship of the line by passing her at sea while going backwards.[*]

---

[*] For more information, please see my book, *The Oasis Sisters: Royal Caribbean's Fleet of the World's Biggest Cruise Ships*, available online in both e-Book and paperback versions.

Bibliography and Further Reading

Books

Arnott, Captain Robert, *Captain of the Queen* (New English Library, 1982).

Ballard, Robert, *Lost Liners* (Hyperion Books, 1998).

Bisset, Commodore James, *Commodore* (Angus & Robertson, 1961).

Bond, Geoffrey, *Lakonia* (Oldbourne Book Co., 1966).

Curtis, Paul, *Aboard Pacific Princess* (Rose Publishing, 2019).

Curtis, Paul, *High Tea on the Cunard Queens* (The History Press, 2019).

Curtis, Paul, *The Oasis Sisters* (Rose Publishing, 2019).

De Silva, Rocha, *My Way to the Seven Seas* (Renbro, 2015).

Frame, Chris, *Evolution of the Transatlantic Liner* (The History Press, 2011).

Frame, Chris, *The Cunard Story* (The History Press, 2022).

Gladstone, Eugene W., *In the Wake of the Andrea Doria* (McClelland & Stewart, 1966).

Kepler, Thomas, *The Ile de France and the Golden Age of Transatlantic Travel: High Style on the High Seas* (Lyons Press, 2021).

Lord, Walter, *A Night to Remember* (Griffen, 2005).

MacLean, Commodore Dan, *Queens' Company* (Hutchinson, 1965).

Marr, Commodore Geoffrey, *The Queen and I* (Coles, 1973).

McCart, Neil, *SS Canberra* (Waterfront Publications, 1989).

Miller, William H., *SS France/Norway* (The History Press, 2009).

Miller, William H., *SS Nieuw Amsterdam* (Amberley Publishing, 2010).

Plowman, Piers, and Stephen J. Card, *Queen of Bermuda and the Furness Bermuda Line* (Bermuda Maritime, 2002).

Potter, Neil, and Jack Frost, *Queen Elizabeth* (Harrap, 1969).

Potter, Neil, and Jack Frost, *Queen Elizabeth 2* (Harrap, 1969).

Potter, Neil, and Jack Frost, *Queen Mary* (San Francisco Press, 1971).

Thelwell, Commodore Robert G., *I Captained the Big Ships* (Baker, 1961).

Treasure-Jones, Captain John, *Tramp to Queen* (Tempus, 2008).

Warwick, Commodore Ronald, *QE2* (Norton, 1994).

Newspapers

Chicago Tribune (court reports on SS *Eastland*).
Herald and Examiner (Jack Woolford reports on SS *Eastland*).
New York Times (*Costa Concordia* and RMS *Caronia* reports).
Washington Post (Sigonella Crisis).
Weekly Illustrated (reports of RMS *Mauretania*'s maiden voyage).

Websites

www.marinefirefighting.com
www.newspaperarchive.com (news reports on all issues).
www.wikipedia.org
The websites of Cunard, Holland America Line and Royal Caribbean.
www.ojp.gov/ncjrs/virtual-library/abstracts/extradition-and-united-states-prosecution-achille-lauro-hostage (MS *Achille Lauro* hijacking).
https://ir.lawnet.fordham.edu/cgi/viewcontent.cgi?referer=&httpsredir=1&article=1123&context=ilj (MS *Achille Lauro* hijacking).
www.britannica.com (SS *Andrea Doria* reports).
www.nytimes.com/1969/03/11/archives/explosion-halts-caribias-cruise-engineroom-blast-forces-line-to.html (RMS *Caronia* explosion).
www.cbsnews.com/news/cruise-captain-sparks-outrage-among-mariners/ (*Costa Concordia*).
www.latimes.com/travel/la-tr-insider-20120122-story.html (*Costa Concordia*).
www.latimes.com/world/la-xpm-2013-oct-29-la-fg-wn-dancer-lover-costa-concordia-captain-20131029-story.html (*Costa Concordia*).
www.mitma.gob.es/recursos_mfom/2012costaconcordia.pdf (*Costa Concordia* investigation).
https://military-history.fandom.com/wiki/SS_Eastland (SS *Eastland*).
https://estonianworld.com/security/swedish-defence-forces-ms-estonia-transported-military-equipment/ (MS *Estonia*).
https://news.err.ee/1140442/head-of-ms-estonia-investigation-estonia-sank-on-collision-with-submarine (MS *Estonia*).
https://onse.fi/estonia/conten.html (MS *Estonia*).
www.theguardian.com/world/2022/sep/05/film-makers-found-guilty-of-disturbing-1994-ms-estonia-ferry-wreck (MS *Estonia*).
www.bbc.com (MS *Estonia* court reports).
www.nytimes.com/2020/09/30/world/europe/estonia-ferry-disaster-documentary.html (MS *Estonia* documentary).
www.theguardian.com/world/2023/jan/23/estonia-ferry-disaster-inquiry-backs-finding-bow-door-was-to-blame (MS *Estonia* inquiry).
www.yle.Fi (MS *Estonia* murder acquitted).
www.nbcnews.com/id/wbna12702721 (SS *France* asbestos).
www.france24.com/en/20080211-eight-cleared-queen-mary-disaster-accident-trial (RMS *Queen Mary 2* gangway collapse).
www reuters.com (Sigonella Crisis).
https://unsungscience.com/news/back-to-titanic-part-1/ (RMS *Titanic*).
www.ssusc.org/news (SS *United States*).

Acknowledgements

Thanks to Stephen J. Card for allowing a black and white reproduction of his colour painting of *Queen of Bermuda*.

Thanks also to James A. Flood for allowing the black and white reproduction of his beautiful painting of *SS Normandie*. If you like paintings of cruise ships you should visit www.jamesaflood.com for an absolute treasure trove of pictures of great ocean liners.

I also received help from Vincent Sapaen and a couple of excellent Facebook groups. I particularly recommend Ocean Liners and More by Foxstar and QM1 Restore the Queen. The story of Frank Prentice on *Titanic* is based on a filmed interview in the BBC archives. With regard to the use of photos of older ships, I have made every reasonable attempt to find the true copyright holder, if any. If you see an omission, please let me know. I feel it is important to help see that an author's work is protected.

My thanks also go to my family for supporting me through my various idiosyncrasies. These should probably best go unpublished.

I feel I should also acknowledge or even admit, by the number of its ships included, I could be showing a hint of bias in favour of Cunard. The honour of my own time with them as an entertainment officer was relatively brief. But in that time, I admit to having gained a healthy respect for its traditions and loyalties. However, the number of its ships included is purely based on the company's long history and its large number of significant ships. I assure my reader they stopped paying me in 1967.

Most importantly, I would like to thank my diligent friends at The History Press for their encouragement to again finish a manuscript. They are commissioning editor Amy Rigg and project editor Alex Boulton.

I would particularly like to thank the financial department of The History Press. They are the ones who send me the royalties!

Last, but not least, I wish you, dear reader, fair winds and following seas.

About the Author

The author.

As a boy, Paul Curtis sailed small boats on the Solent, watching with fascination the endless procession of liners and cruise ships coming and going to countries across the world.

It set him dreaming. How exciting they seemed: top sides gleaming, passengers lining the rails and smoke puffing purposely from their funnels as they stemmed the tide between the south of England and the Isle of Wight.

While other kids were off trainspotting, Paul was learning all about the ships, which ports they were visiting and who were these passengers on their life-changing journey. Most of all, he dreamt what life must be like both on board and in the ports visited.

Before he was 18, he managed to get a job on a passenger liner: first as a ship's photographer and later as a ship's entertainment officer.

After working on ten different ships, he swallowed the anchor, but his love of the life at sea never dimmed. At every opportunity, he is off on passenger ships, or anything else that floats.

This is his fifth book about ships, all written with a dash of humour and whimsy.

Paul's website contains further information on passenger ships: www.paulcurtis.com.au. Paul enjoys hearing from his readers and can be contacted at paul@paulcurtis.com.au.